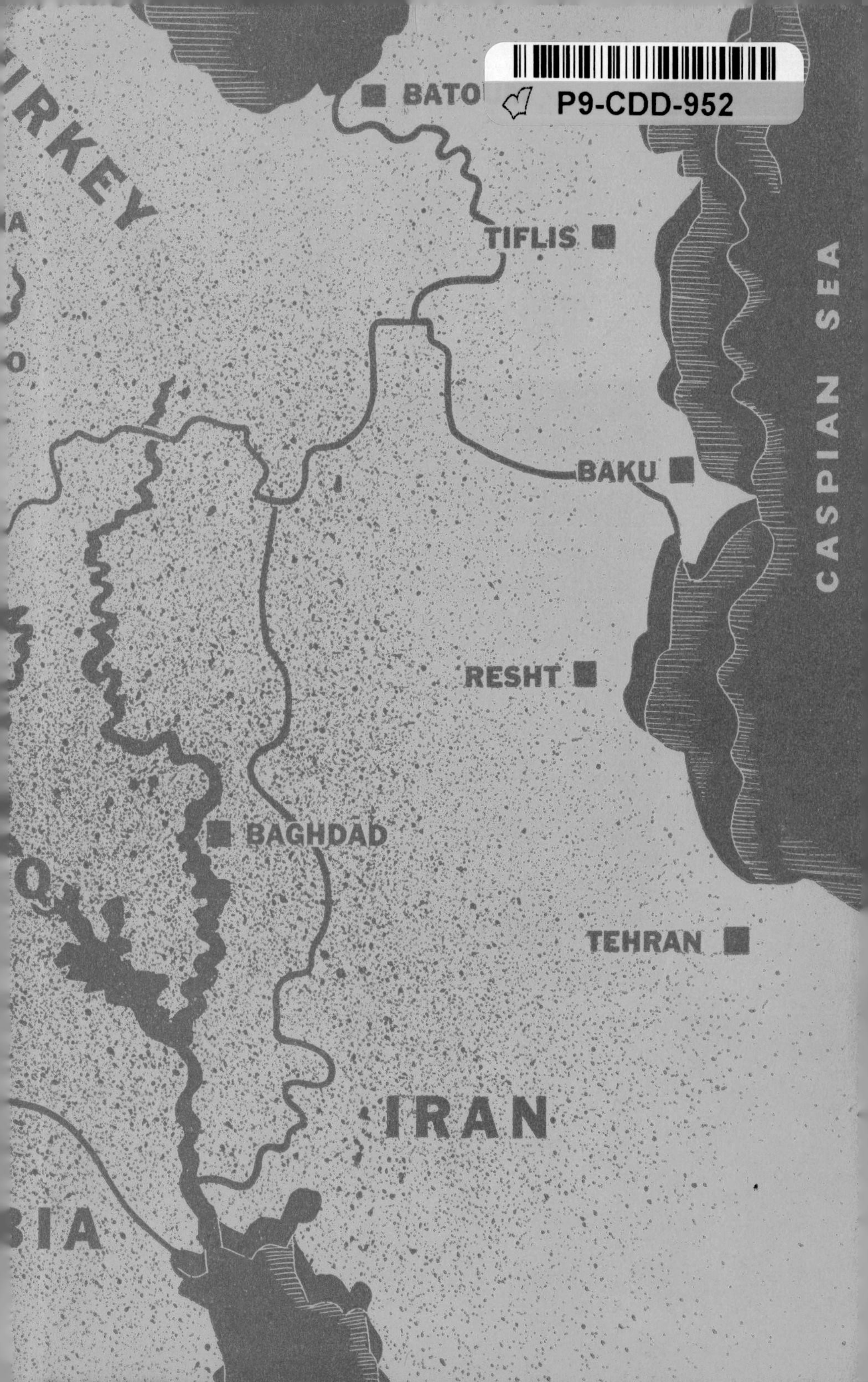

P9-CDD-952
IRKEY
BATO
TIFLIS
CASPIAN SEA
BAKU
RESHT
BAGHDAD
TEHRAN
IRAN
BIA

GERTRUDE BELL

By RONALD BODLEY and LORNA HEARST

Gertrude Bell, who with T. E. Lawrence and Sir Percy Cox created the kingdom of Iraq, was a remarkable woman. To wealth and position she added wit, intelligence and good looks. Despite the conventions of the 1890's, she excelled in mountain climbing, in modern history at Oxford, and in writing both prose and verse.

After she had been presented at court, a visit to relatives in the British legation at Tehran roused what became an unquenchable love of the East. So Gertrude Bell studied Persian and Arabic and organized private caravans to explore unknown desert regions. As an amateur she visited native tribes, whose chiefs became her firm friends. She learned desert customs, made maps, delved into history and archaeology. Then a short period in the Arab Bureau and a visit to the viceroy of India were preliminary steps to an appointment in Mesopotamia which, in various guises, she retained to the day of her death. There she and Lawrence and Sir Percy slowly began the organization of Iraq, which culminated in the coronation of Faisal in 1921. For the rest of her life she stayed on in Baghdad, lending a hand in countless problems, religious and political, between Arabs and English.

Her biography is a tale of exploration and adventure and of almost incredible achievement.

THE MACMILLAN COMPANY
NEW YORK · BOSTON · CHICAGO · DALLAS
ATLANTA · SAN FRANCISCO

MACMILLAN AND CO., LIMITED
LONDON · BOMBAY · CALCUTTA · MADRAS
MELBOURNE

THE MACMILLAN COMPANY
OF CANADA, LIMITED
TORONTO

GERTRUDE BELL

by

Ronald Bodley

and

Lorna Hearst

New York

THE MACMILLAN COMPANY

1940

Set up and printed. Published November, 1940.

FIRST PRINTING.

PRINTED IN THE UNITED STATES OF AMERICA
AMERICAN BOOK–STRATFORD PRESS, INC., NEW YORK

TO

EVELYN BODLEY-HUNT
(née Evelyn Bell)

FOREWORD

A biographer who undertakes to write the life of a relative is apt to find himself viewing his subject from too close a perspective, but though Gertrude Bell's father was my grandfather's brother, circumstances gave me little opportunity of knowing her. It was more the setting in which she passed her life than her personality which first tempted me to write about her.

My maternal grandfather, Gertrude's uncle, lived for many years in Arab surroundings, and through this connection I was brought at an early age into touch with the Arabs and later on spent seven years among the nomads of the desert. During this period I became intimately acquainted with the country, living with the Bedouins in their tents, sharing their food and learning as much about them as it is possible for an Occidental to learn about an Oriental. Gertrude like myself felt the charm of the desert and appreciated the Arab mentality. She penetrated behind the Moslem reserve and felt herself liked by a race which instinctively resents the non-Mohammedan. To a lesser degree I created an intimacy with the desert peoples which has explained many things in Gertrude's life, otherwise obscure.

At the same time this bond in common and knowledge of the subject's background has not been entirely an advantage in writing the biography. Being too close to the picture is apt to make one slur over the small details of desert life which would be new and interesting to readers unacquainted with the ways of the Arabs. The great Anglo-Arab scholar, H. St. J. Philby, says in his book *Sheba's Daughters* that "writing about Arabia is like talking to oneself without an audience; so few people know the ground and it is so hard to know what to explain and what not to explain . . ."

Bearing this in mind, therefore, I have tried to tell of the desert as if it were new to me, to convey that sensation of immensity and desolation which no painter or photographer has been able to reproduce, and, at the same time, to show the Arabs as they really are.

RONALD BODLEY

INTRODUCTION

The famous explorers and administrators who set out from Europe during the sixteenth and seventeenth centuries to open unknown parts of the world to white men were pioneers of great courage. They discovered new continents, they set up new empires, they charted unknown seas and unheard of lands, but they did so with the aid of the sword and usually with the ulterior motive of material gain.

Gertrude Bell mapped great areas of unexplored territory, she was instrumental in establishing a new kingdom, she created a better understanding between the people of the Near East and the Occident, but she gained nothing by it but the collapse of her health which brought about her death in the midst of her work. The hardest task for Gertrude Bell's biographer is not to underestimate what she achieved.

Unlike many explorers who went on their expeditions backed by governments or scientific societies, Gertrude Bell was, until the latter part of her life, completely alone. She organized her own caravans, paid for them with her own money and departed into wildernesses knowing that if she disappeared no one would come to look for her. In order to appreciate her journeys the atmosphere in which she travelled must be constantly borne in mind. One must think of her all alone with her Arabs, setting out over those grim wastes of stones and sands with nothing to support her but the determination to reach her goal. One must remember that attitude towards the "infidel" of the Moslem who has that ineradicable certainty that the only people who are worthy of respect and can have any hope of future salvation are the followers of Mohammed. If this were not sufficient handicap to someone who had decided to make her life among Moslems, Gertrude Bell had an even greater one in being of a sex looked down upon by the followers of the Prophet. But instead of letting this be a hindrance she put it to every advantage to gain her ends, and this feminine creature, who had the will power of a man, became a legendary figure, loved and respected from the Red Sea to the Persian Gulf.

We take this opportunity to thank those who have helped us in the making of the book.

Mrs. H. L. Hunt, mother of Major Bodley and Gertrude Bell's cousin; Sir Maurice Bell, Gertrude's brother; and Lady Richmond, Gertrude's step-sister, who revised the original manuscript and supplied interesting material about Gertrude's life.

Ruth Collier, who also read the manuscript and criticised it from the point of view of the American public.

And Frances Manson, who pointed out what an original subject Gertrude Bell's life offered for a book.

CONTENTS

PART I

GIRLHOOD

CHAPTER I

THE SUN TOUCHED THE HORIZON and set behind the Durham moorlands. A blackcock called and the grouse settled closer into the heather—the time was drawing near when their only respite from the guns would be at night. A fox lifted his head and cocked an ear; he had a little longer peace than the grouse before the hounds would be after him again. A quick afterglow, which faded almost at once, followed the sunset, and the night breeze went hissing through the brush.

Along a dusty road, white in the twilight, a gamekeeper came trudging. He had that sturdy build and determined look in his eyes which has given to the North Countrymen of Britain the reputation of being the hardiest race in the world. As he reached the crest of the road he paused and turned towards the west. Sunsets over these wild moorlands were not new to him, but they still fascinated him. Until the sun disappeared the country was all green and mauve and brown, but once it had gone the landscape became a great rolling, colourless expanse. It reminded him of the desert.

He smiled reminiscently. Only those who had served Britain in the East would understand this simile . . . The desert . . . The gamekeeper looked up expecting almost to see an Arab on his camel or an Indian Sowar riding up the road. But the darkening landscape was deserted and silent except for the hissing of the wind.

The man shrugged his shoulders and walked on.

Ten years now since the Great Mutiny—nearly twelve since those days of horror besieged in Lucknow and those hours of triumphal revenge, storming the Kashmir Gate at Delhi . . . fourteen years since the Battle of the Alma . . . funny how the Durham moorlands reminded him of those countries—India—the Crimea . . .

It was now quite dark and the glare of the furnaces of the iron foundries could be seen flickering against the sky—it might be Cawnpore burning or the campfires of the armies before Inkerman. There was some connection too, for without the foundries of Bell Brothers, wars could not be fought, ships could not cross the oceans, England could not exist. Bell Brothers kept those furnaces in the North Country alive and made it possible for Britons to conquer the world. Lowthian Bell, Hugh Bell, John Bell and their servant the gamekeeper were all parts of the great empire-building machine.

A bend in the road brought the gamekeeper suddenly to a property, through the surrounding trees of which he could see the lights of a house twinkling. His own cottage was a little farther down the road, but he decided to call in at Washington Hall and pass the time of day with the servants of the Bell household. The head coachman and the gamekeeper had been soldiers together in India and he felt in the mood to "sling the bat." [1] As he crunched up the drive he noticed that the upper part of the Hall had brighter lights than usual and several carriages, as well as the local

[1] Soldiers' slang; Hindustani idiom for swapping yarns.

doctor's gig, waited outside the entrance. The gamekeeper walked round to the back and into the kitchen, but instead of finding the sedate atmosphere, which was customary at this hour of the day, everyone seemed to be scurrying about or talking in whispers. The gamekeeper joined a group of servants who muttered in a corner, and was about to inquire what it was all about when the door of the kitchen opened and the butler came in. The maids glanced apprehensively at the august figure, but the butler's demeanour maintained the unruffled exterior of the descendant of generations of gentlemen's servants. He looked about him importantly, nodded to the gamekeeper and, clearing his throat, said:

"Mrs. Bell has given birth to a daughter . . . Mr. Lowthian is now a grandfather . . ."

The wind had dropped when the gamekeeper left the Hall and the stars shone so brightly that they seemed to be quite close to the earth. The moorlands looked more and more like the desert, and the gamekeeper had a feeling of crowds about him. He shook himself and blinked his eyes, but do what he might he could not escape from that sensation of hosts of robed people bringing with them all the odours of the Orient, as they seethed over the Durham moors and swept past the home of the newborn child . . .

Gertrude Bell was born on July 14, 1868, at Washington Hall in the county of Durham, the home of her grandfather, Lowthian Bell.

Lowthian Bell, a great figure of Victorian England, was, in addition to being the mind behind the growing iron industry of the North of England, a distinguished man of science. Gertrude's father, Hugh, was Sir Lowthian's eldest son; her mother was Mary Shield, daughter of John Shield of Newcastle on Tyne. Gertrude, therefore, inherited all that energy and tenacity of the people of the North. Her mother died when she was three years old which, no doubt, had much to do with the moulding of her independent nature.

Although the birth of Gertrude Bell on that summer's night created no more stir than the birth of any other daughter of an English country gentleman, her advent into the world was to have far-reaching effects on the British Empire.

It was before the days when Kipling had made British Imperialism a subject for stirring ballads—"Take hold of the wings of the morning and flop round the world till you're dead . . ." was beginning to be an accomplished fact, but was not yet appreciated by the general public.

British generals and statesmen went about their business in a matter-of-fact way, subduing, developing, educating the countries in distant parts of the world which seemed ripe to become "the white man's burden." The telegraph and the telephone had not linked up continents to any practical degree, and the news of new conquests was not recorded until the Union Jack had been hoisted and "Rule Britannia" added to the musical repertoire of the black, yellow or brown adoptions of the great white queen. The other nations of the world had their own domestic problems or were too busy empire building to worry about the doings of their neighbours. Practical democracy was in its infancy, a journey to India or America was a serious undertaking and the idea of challenging Britain's rule of the sea had not been dreamed of. True that wars were brewing on the continent of Europe, but they were not the business of the British, provided they did not interfere with their commerce.

It was a comparatively pleasant world to be born into for such as Gertrude Bell. Her family was wealthy and stood for the Imperial policies of Queen Victoria's government. Her life would continue in the atmosphere of County respectability, governesses would come and go until she was considered educated and could grow up to join in the usual round of English life of her class. Fox hunting in the winter, grouse shooting in the autumn, the London Season in the summer and an occasional visit to some Continental resort. Those were the plans, plans which ninety-nine per cent of young ladies of Gertrude's breeding would relentlessly follow till their deaths. Luckily, however, for England, Gertrude belonged to the one per cent which shows that the exception proves the rule.

Five years after the death of Gertrude's mother, her father married Florence Olliffe, the daughter of Sir Joseph Olliffe. She was herself a brilliant woman and a writer of many plays and books. The relationship between step-mother and daughter was of the most intimate and it is to Florence Bell that we owe the main facts of her remarkable step-daughter's life, recorded in the famous series of letters which were preserved and later published.

To the outside world, Gertrude is chiefly known for what she did in Britain's service in the East. There are many, in fact, who picture her as a kind of man, with a female anatomy, shouldering the white man's burden in the far-flung confines of the British Empire. Nothing could be less exact, for, while Gertrude's rôle as an administratrix will be handed down through history, she was many other things.

Primarily, Gertrude was an exceedingly feminine woman. She had charm and good looks and in the midst of her wildest adventures kept the instincts of her sex foremost in her mind. It was probably more this instinct than anything else, combined with her force of character, which carried her along to success. Gertrude understood how to handle men, but the handling was not that of an authoritative officer but of a woman who knew that men, of whatever race or age, are fundamentally weak when dealing with a beautiful and attractive woman. She always took trouble with her clothes and, whether she was living on the banks of the Thames or the Tigris, she always turned out better dressed than anyone else. In the midst of a trek over the desert or the solving of a dry administrative problem, she would be writing home for some article of feminine apparel or discussing a subject dear only to women.

Gertrude had so many interests that had she not followed her distinguished career she would never have been bored. One of her chief hobbies was gardening and the rock garden which she planned at Rounton Grange, her Yorkshire home, became one of the show-places of England. She studied natural history, wrote poetry even better than she wrote prose, was a first class historian and archaeologist, could climb a Swiss crag with the same lack of fuss as she would cross an unmapped desert and come home to discuss art with the best art critics of the day. She also found time to play and there was no one who loved society more than Gertrude. Fox hunting, she was an expert horsewoman;

games, parties, dancing, all came into Gertrude's life and were enjoyed with as much enthusiasm as the more serious pursuits. Every asset which birth can give and a greater proportion of physical gifts than usually fall to one person were hers, but there was never the slightest attitude that she was in any way superior to the average woman of her time.

At an early age Gertrude showed that spirit which was to lead her into a life of adventure and there were wild escapades in the grounds of her home with her younger brother Maurice, the present baronet. She had her ponies and the assortment of pets dear to all children. In the schoolroom governesses taught the orthodox subjects which Gertrude assimilated without much trouble and no violent enthusiasm. Her nature was extremely independent and she resented discipline from those who could not enforce it. Nothing pleased her more than to defy a governess until the harassed woman was obliged to resort to parental authority. Even when her step-mother intervened Gertrude would only grudgingly and temporarily admit the rule of the teacher.

Gertrude developed mountaineering instincts when still a child. She usually spent part of the summer holidays with cousins in Scotland. A letter written at the age of twelve describes her first climb.

". . . On Friday we all fished. We fished up a burn with a worm, Maurice caught two trout and I caught one. We had our shoes and stockings off all the morning. In the afternoon we went a beautiful drive and we left the carriage at an inn and went a long walk and got lots of beautiful heather, flowers and cotton-grass, if you know what that is. I climbed up a very steep rock which had very little to hold on by and when I got nearly to the top I could not get any further and I could not get down. Aunty Florence got up round the side and tried to reach me with her parasol, but she could not. At last I got down and I was very glad . . ."

Combined with this taste for adventure was a more peaceful love of gardening and reading. Her gift for letter writing became apparent when she was still very young, and the famous correspondence of maturer years was preceded by childhood letters which are clearly expressed and most amusing. There are accounts of trips to Scotland, analyses of books by Harrison Ainsworth and the letters of Carlyle and Mozart, the progress of a collection of birds' eggs, with a few business-like barters with cousins, and a description of Mr. Gladstone addressing a mass meeting in Leeds in 1882. She played what she calls "raquettes" against the door of the coach house and speaks with disparagement of having to study the piano which she could never master, in spite of having a taste for music.

Such was Gertrude's childhood with all the usual tragedies and joys in the lives of normal children and all in a background of serene family life which so many young people of the present day lack. A background of great beauty too, in a home designed by Philip Webb and decorated by William Morris and Burne-Jones.

It was not until Maurice had gone to Eton that Gertrude's education took a serious turn when, at the age of fifteen, she was sent to an "academy for young ladies" in London.

It was not customary in 1883 for girls of Gertrude's class to be sent away to school, but Mrs. Bell felt that her stepdaughter had a mind and a character which needed something more forceful than a private governess. The school chosen was Queen's College in London over which a friend of Mrs. Bell presided. Gertrude did not like leaving home and, while philosophically settling down to her daily routine, she was homesick at the beginning of each new term.

Maturity came quickly to her and, in her sixteenth year, her thoughts were in advance of those of the average schoolgirl. Clothes were taking their place in her life, opinions of people were developing, boys were no longer playmates to be outrivalled in the climbing of trees, and that determined character which was to shape her future career was making itself even more evident. The pretty child with red-gold hair and sea-blue eyes had become a beautiful girl with an attractive figure which she kept until her death.

One of the first events of importance in Gertrude's school life was her confirmation. The immediate reaction was a number of good resolutions, followed by her first communion which also caused a passing impression. Religion, however, never played any real part in Gertrude's life, and while for a time she attended church she could never be convinced that any particular faith would help her.

London brought her into contact with interesting men and women whom she accepted at their face value, being less impressed by social position than by personality. Great names meant hardly anything to her, and when her grandfather was created a baronet she wrote confidentially to her father to say that, while congratulating Sir Lowthian, she wished that he had been able to refuse the title. It was probably through Gertrude's influence that, in later years, her father twice refused a peerage.

She met Jenny Lind but was more attracted to another

actress, Fanny Kemble, the niece of Mrs. Siddons. The American doctor, Weir Mitchell, who invented "the rest cure" made her feel fidgety, while the personality of Mrs. Humphry Ward soothed her. One day her mother introduced her to Robert Browning and she was "immensely interested"!

She started going regularly to the theatre and attended the first night of *The Mikado* with Arthur Sullivan conducting. She was taken to the Albert Hall to witness a performance of *Faust* which was still regarded as hardly suitable for "jeunes filles"! She began to take dancing lessons and was one of the first to learn the Hop Waltz which had been inspired by the new tempos of the young Strauss. It was considered very modern to do the Hop Waltz and young men still asked their partners if they would "slide or hop it"!

Her love of music developed with that of dancing, combined with that still fierce dislike of studying the piano. It gave her no pleasure to play and she naturally concluded that her presence at the piano must cause pain and grief to others. However, some years passed before she could persuade Mrs. Bell that this supposedly necessary accomplishment for a fashionable young lady of that period could be dispensed with. Paradoxically, she liked singing and had a sufficiently good voice to make her teachers feel that it was worth developing. As a matter of fact most of Gertrude's elaborate education was never to be of any practical value to her and courses in political economy and Oriental law would have served her much better.

These protests against learning the piano were further signs of the independent character which was to be the outstanding trait in the whole of Gertrude's life. She still had the respectful Victorian attitude of daughters towards their parents and automatically asked permission of her stepmother to do things, about which girls of today would consult no one, but, if she considered the parental authority unreasonable, she had no hesitation in saying so. Even when the question of employing expressions of mild slang in letters met with disapproval they were received with an immediate remonstrance:

> "I think that it is priggish to say—in excellent health," she wrote to Mrs. Bell in reply to a letter admonishing her for laxity in her English, "—my own expression may be slang but it is infinitely preferable, I think. Would you have me say when talking of the sovereign, the Queen of England, Scotland, Ireland, Empress of India, Defender of the Faith? If not, why not the National, for the National Gallery? My life is not long enough to give everything its full title."

With her father Gertrude discussed politics. She was and remained always a Liberal and a Gladstonian. Parnell was at the height of his power and had instituted boycotting and intimidation in Ireland to enforce his demands for Home Rule. Gertrude followed these political controversies with clear logical reasoning, far in advance of her years. She had no ideas about taking up politics herself and her interest was lively and detached, admiring Mr. Gladstone as she would Cromwell or Cavour. She, nevertheless, had those instinctive qualities of statesmanship which were to make her, thirty years later, into a great administratrix of a country not her own.

With her interest in politics, her aptitude for history was becoming apparent and it was clear to her professors that she would soon pass beyond the standard of their teaching. At the end of 1885 she had broached to her father the possibility of her going to Cambridge, but in the spring of 1886 she decided definitely that she would complete her studies at Oxford. Having settled this matter in her crisp, determined way, she dismissed it for the time being and spent the Easter holidays walking through Devonshire, scaling cliffs and deep sea fishing, as if the question of her education held no place in her existence.

This is a remarkable trait in Gertrude's mental outlook which repeated itself again and again in her life. Throughout her adventures in Arabia, during her excavations and while kingdom-making in Iraq, she was always able to divorce herself from serious matters and give herself up wholeheartedly to sport or social pleasures. It was the secret of her energy and success. Statesmen, university professors, big game hunters, young men about town, thought of her as fitting into their modes of living and their way of thinking and would have vehemently denied that she had any other life than such as theirs!

CHAPTER II

In the May term of 1886 Gertrude went up to Lady Margaret Hall at Oxford. She was not quite eighteen, and the youthful enthusiasm which sparkled in her eyes made people forget that behind that charming exterior there was a brilliant brain.

To have a girl of Gertrude's background educated at a school away from home was a departure from the normal, but to send a young lady to the University was quite exceptional. Somerville and Lady Margaret Hall, the two colleges for women, had only been functioning for seven years and were regarded by the older generation of dons as an undermining influence to their time-honoured and sacred traditions. The Oxford of those days was nearer to the Tractarian Oxford than to the modern university. Doctor Jowett still presided at Balliol and Lewis Carroll could be seen daily walking across the quadrangle of Christ Church. It was not so long since Rhodes had left Oriel to build an empire in South Africa and Ruskin had lectured on art at the Sheldonian Theatre. Herkomer still guided the budding careers of young painters, and Oscar Wilde was remembered for his epigrams but not yet known as a writer.

It was an Oxford of cobbled pavings which resounded to the clatter of dog carts driven by undergraduates; the streets were lit by gas and young gentlemen wined and dined in the mellow light of candles in silver candelabra. The motor car was a long way off as a practical means of locomotion; the telephone was hardly known; submarines, aircraft, radio, were fantastic ideas in the minds of scoffed-at dreamers. The only two republics of importance were those of the United States and France and students of history could find first-hand knowledge of the governments of other countries which had little changed during the preceding centuries.

It was a dignified Oxford which did not yet know the colonial scholar or the radical agitator. It was a rural Oxford, a mediaeval city, surrounded by fields and meadows from which, as an Anglican citadel, the Catholic was excluded by pontifical decree. It was an Oxford into which the women's colleges had come as a preliminary wedge to shake its ancient foundations and lose it its secluded charm.

But although women had officially invaded Oxford, the conventions governing the relationship between male and female students were even stricter than those applied to the sexes outside a university. A girl alone might not go out into the street, and at lectures which men attended the undergraduettes were accompanied by a chaperon and sat at a safe distance from the undergraduates. Horace Marshall, Gertrude's first cousin who had practically been brought up with her, was at Trinity, but when the two young people first met they had to behave almost as if they were strangers. In a letter to her step-mother Gertrude confessed that she took a stroll with Horace in the Park and hoped that she would not mind. Later the principal of Lady Margaret authorized discreet walks with Horace but, apart from this concession, Gertrude never spoke to a fellow undergraduate except at a dance or in the company of other girls. It seems incredible that so prudish a mentality should have existed such a short time ago or that Gertrude, who was later to live entirely in the company of men, should have submitted to this tyranny. But she did it because it was the custom of the time and, although she occasionally revolted, she found it difficult to strike out on a new line which had no precedent. Her mind was imbued with Victorian principles and she was one day slightly shocked at meeting a girl who had but lately married and was wearing a hat instead of the conventional bonnet decreed for those who had abandoned spinsterhood!

In spite of this sentiment she was considered by some as being rather advanced in her ideas. To others she gave an impression of primness which was probably due to her not being over-expansive. She knew what she wanted, she knew the kind of people she wished to know and she did not make friends on sight. The day of nicknames and "darling" used promiscuously had not come, and Gertrude addressed formally all those whom she met until a real intimacy had developed. During practically the whole of her first term at Oxford she never spoke or referred to a girl without the prefix "Miss." When she did employ Christian names it meant that a real and lasting friendship had begun, and there were many at Oxford who remained Gertrude's intimates all her life.

Prominent among these was Janet Hogarth, who was to be strangely linked with Gertrude's destinies through her brother David Hogarth, the famous archaeologist and Orientalist. Years later Hogarth and Gertrude were to collaborate in Arabia and it was due to Hogarth that she found herself in 1915 launched on her career of empire building while, through the same influence, T. E. Lawrence was leading the Arabs in revolt.

Little by little a circle of intimate friends formed about Gertrude, and before her first year at the university was completed she had become a factor in the life of Oxford women. Most females who become prominent at institutions of learning base their reputations on mental brilliance, many on their achievements in the playing fields, a few on saintliness. Gertrude was not saintly, she played games sufficiently well to enjoy herself and she could hold her own with the great majority of her fellow students in the classroom. But her initial prominence at Oxford was for none of these reasons and belonged to a branch of university life entirely feminine and remote from the curriculum. Gertrude was developing a taste for dress.

Paradoxically, she was not a needlewoman, although she turned out the usual horrors of that era in the shape of cushion covers and fire screens. She knitted shapeless sweaters for male relatives and socks which caused blisters to the wearers, but as she grew older she gradually abandoned all forms of sewing as a painful and futile occupation.

Gertrude had the clothes instinct, but at the back of her mind there was the appreciation of their psychological importance and effect on certain situations. During her final examinations at Oxford she appeared in a different gown every day. It is not suggested that her physical charms affected examiners, but even professors have some male instincts left; and, if two candidates of equal merit come up to be questioned and there is doubt as to the awarding of the higher mark, the little feminine something may weigh just that much in the balance.

Gertrude did more, however, than actually dress well, she set a mode which lasted. Female footwear was still of the boot variety and Gertrude introduced brown low-cut shoes as more comfortable and practical.

These feminine traits appeared also in her attitude towards the emancipation of women which was advocated by the majority of the undergraduates. She treated the college debates on the subject as a joke, maintaining always that women were women and only in exceptional cases fitted to take on the responsibilities of men. A strange attitude from one who was to become one of the world's first stateswomen!

Again, paradoxically, Gertrude began to smoke cigarettes before she was twenty. Ladies of that day did not smoke and the cigarette in female lips was the monopoly of the chorus girl and her kind. Smoking was regarded as fast and unwomanly, and in many houses the men were relegated to a special room set aside for the specific purpose of indulging in this malodorous occupation. But Gertrude decided that she wanted to smoke, so she began in her teens and informed her parents that she had done so, with a plea that they should not mind.

This feminine and independent attitude did not prevent her from taking an active part in the outdoor amusements of Oxford. The playing of games by women was not general in 1886 and the females who excelled at sports were expected to have rough, red complexions and huge, bony hands. Gertrude proved that these outward characteristics were not necessary. She swam, she rowed, she played tennis and even hockey. Her favourite game was tennis, at which she excelled; she won her college tournament, thereby being selected to represent Lady Margaret and having the chance to play for the University. She attended all the sporting contests of the Varsity teams with a critical knowledge of good rowing or bad cricket.

The religious side of an English university, which plays a daily and prominent part in the life of an undergraduate, interested her from an objective point of view. The dramatic sermons of the Bishop of Ripon to packed congregations of eager young men and women impressed her more for the oratorical powers of the preacher than the message which he was trying to convey. Before she left Oxford, Gertrude had decided that there was no particular creed in which she would like to put her trust and she lived and died without any determined religion.

She joined in the college theatricals and went through all the trials which are the happy lot of amateurs putting on plays. Leading parts were assigned to her but, although her step-mother was a distinguished playwright, Gertrude had little enthusiasm for the theatre. Her attitude towards life was to sample everything until the occupation or pastime which interested her most had been discovered.

She attended debates at the Union and heard young Coningsby Disraeli speak against Home Rule, and T. P. O'Connor, who was the guest of the evening, keep the "house" in an uproar of laughter and applause replying to the nephew of the great prime minister. She spoke at her college debating society, but had not the mentality of a politician and disliked making speeches.

It was during her time at Oxford that she made her first trip outside the British Isles and visited rural Germany where she found difficulty in adapting herself to unusual conditions of living. In fact she showed the most insular mentality during these Oxford days with no indication that other peoples of the world would ever interest her.

What Gertrude did approach with enthusiasm were her studies. Her mind was superior to the majority of her contemporaries and she could hold her own intellectually with men like the "great Mr. Murray"—Professor Gilbert Murray to be. But although she was conscientious about her classes and took her work more seriously than many of her colleagues she never allowed anyone to become over-aware of her intelligence, and the success which crowned her final examinations was a surprise to her circle. She was simply a popular girl full of the fun of exuberant youth and few suspected that her Oxford career would end in literary triumph.

During Commemoration Week, when all those who aspired to honours in the examinations studied to the last minute and went to bed early, Gertrude danced to all hours of the morning and appeared in the lecture halls, fresh as a daffodil. There was no trace of nervousness in her behaviour and, at her "viva voce," when confronted with the eminent historian, S. R. Gardiner, the great authority on English history of the seventeenth century, she did not wait for his questions and opened the attack with:

"I am afraid, Professor Gardiner, that I must differ from your estimate of Charles I . . ."

When Gertrude left Oxford in 1888 she had passed all her examinations with distinction and taken a brilliant first class in modern history.

Thus finished an Oxford career which had been as successful as it had been happy. Life seemed to be at Gertrude's feet to do with as she pleased and that life would normally be in the same surroundings in which she had been brought up. There would be none of the uncertainties which today face girls of twenty, and the possibility of international upheavals which might disquiet the majestic progress of late Victorian Britain were not considered. It was an enviable, friendly, careless future to which the lovely young B.A. looked forward.

CHAPTER III

Although Gertrude had specialized in history at Oxford it had not been with any motive other than to satisfy her interest in the subject. She had little practical knowledge of the Continent of Europe and was not particularly anxious to visit it or other parts of the world. The next episode in her life was, however, to be the first link in the chain which was to make of her one of the greatest travellers of her generation.

Gertrude's step-aunt was married to Sir Frank Lascelles, British Minister to Roumania, and as soon as Gertrude left Oxford Lady Lascelles suggested that her niece should spend the winter with her at the legation in Bucharest.

Lady Lascelles belonged to a school of thought which regarded with something akin to distrust highly educated young women who did not have to work for their living, and she felt that a month or so in the gay Roumanian capital would rid Gertrude of some of her "Oxfordy manner." Gertrude was perhaps highly educated, but she never let anyone feel that she had taken honours; and if she had not gone to the University she would have acquired knowledge by some other method. Lady Lascelles soon found out that her niece had no trace of an "Oxfordy manner" and was just as full of the joy of living and eager to have a good time as any girl who had never read a page of history.

Before setting out for the Balkans, Gertrude returned to her home in Yorkshire and immediately set herself to take the "county" into her scheme of life in the same way as she had taken Oxford. She interested herself in housekeeping, and became an active worker among the women of Bell Brothers iron works on the banks of the Tees. In her spare time she taught history to her step-brother and sister, kept up her riding and tennis.

Towards the end of the year she went to London to make ready for her trip to the Continent. Her charm of manner at once made her the centre of friends who found a girl who was just as much at home with a group of serious-minded older people as in a gay ball-room.

In December of 1888 Gertrude left for Paris with her father from which point she was to be escorted to Roumania by Sir Frank Lascelles' eldest son Billy. Of the same age as Gertrude, Billy had just left Sandhurst and was waiting for his commission in the Guards. The two young people had known each other as children and their boy and girl friendship had developed into a flirtation which, at one time, looked as if it might become an engagement. It was Gertrude who came to the conclusion that she was too young to settle down, and allowed the flirtation to continue, as such, with all the thrills of a make-believe love affair. For the moment the young cadet felt exceedingly important at having his cousin entrusted to him for the journey across Europe, and Gertrude very grown up at setting out on her first adventure unchaperoned.

Roumania in 1888 had not the political importance which it acquired in the twentieth century. True that, like all

Balkan states, it was a centre of unrest and a subject of covet by the greater powers which adjoined it, but not for the same reasons as today. Vast oil fields lay beneath the surface of the land, but as there were no motor cars, no airplanes, no oil-driven ships, this wealth was of no practical value except as fuel for lamps. The discovery of the commercial possibilities of oil made Roumania, and, at the same time, lost her much of her peace.

The Bucharest in which Gertrude found herself was a gay city of inconsequent men and women of wealth and social position who thought of little else but enjoying themselves. Life centred round the Court and the foreign legations, and what those who worked in the cities or on the land did or thought was not given much attention by "society." The days when the proletariat would claim any rights to assist in the governing of the country were still remote.

Naturally this first contact with sophisticated men and women was a glorious adventure for Gertrude, although she was not over-impressed by names and judged the people she met by their personal qualities.

Count Goluchowski, who a few years later became the Emperor Francis Joseph's confidential minister of foreign affairs and kept his country on peaceful terms with her neighbours by some of the finest diplomacy in history, was at the Austrian Legation in Bucharest. Gertrude met him at dinner, danced with him, played whist with him and dismissed him as "noisy and rather funny."

Concerning Prince Bülow, who was to succeed Bismarck as Chancellor of the German Empire and to be the progenitor of the Great War, she was quite vague, referring to her first meeting with him among a list of guests as "and Mr. Bülow, who I think is an Austrian diplomat . . . all nice people." Later she conceded that Bülow was the German Minister, but said a great deal more about his beautiful Italian wife.

"Mr. Hardinge a secretary at the British Legation in Constantinople" she liked. Mr. Hardinge liked Gertrude too and they took long walks together, talking unceasingly and oblivious of the dark shadow of Fate which hovered above them. Charles Hardinge was a rising young diplomatist who would eventually become Lord Hardinge of Penshurst and hold the positions of Ambassador in St. Petersburg, Viceroy of India, Ambassador in Paris, and retire into leisured obscurity. It was Hardinge in 1915, while Viceroy of India, who was responsible for the sending of Gertrude to Mesopotamia which launched her on her administrative career and led to the creation of Feisal's kingdom. But at this juncture they were merely young people with interests in common and a mutual admiration.

Gertrude met the Soutzos and the Chrisovelonis and the Marghilomans and other prominent Roumanian families, including Hélène Vacaresco, then a lady-in-waiting at the court and not yet acclaimed as the great poetess. One person impressed her tremendously, the tragic Queen Elizabeth of Roumania, better known to many under the *nom de plume*, under which she wrote, of Carmen Sylva. A beautiful woman, romantic and misunderstood by her stern autocratic husband, she was at once attracted to Gertrude. She had lost her only daughter at the age of four and her poetic soul chafed at the formal, dreary life of the palace. Into Gertrude's ears she poured her romantic ideas which were later to lead her to a semi-disgrace, as a result of helping the intrigue between the heir to the throne of Roumania and her beloved lady-in-waiting, Hélène Vacaresco.

Gertrude arrived in Roumania in time for the family Christmas dinner at the British Legation which ended in a fiasco owing to the rather vague notions in the mind of the Roumanian cook as to how a plum pudding should be cooked. Not realizing that the pudding had to remain in its cloth during the process of boiling, a kind of greasy soup with bits of candied peel and currants floating about was served to the horrified company.

As soon as Christmas was over, Gertrude was swept by her aunt into the gay whirl of the Bucharest winter season. First impressions of "choses vues" are vividly described in letters to Mrs. Bell:

"Aunt Mary and I arrived [at the Soutzos'] at eleven and found the rooms full of people. I was introduced to a great many of them, and danced many turns of the waltz which was going on with different men. This is what happens; your dancer comes up and asks you for a turn. You dance three or four times round the room with him and he then drops you by your chaperon with an elegant bow and someone else comes up and carries you off. You dance nothing through with one person, except the square dances, and in the intervals you either sit with your chaperon or you walk around the rooms with your last partner . . . Far the best dancer in the room was Sztaray, Billy dances very well, Gerald [1] not quite so well, and there was an Austrian who is in the Roumanian army who danced excellently. I believe he is rather a 'Mauvais sujet' really. He fought a duel in Sofia in which he did not behave very well I believe, but he waltzes deliciously. The officers all appear in uniform, of course, with top boots and spurs, but they dance so well that they don't tear one in the least. I was introduced to a great

[1] Gerald Lascelles, Billy's younger brother.

many ladies and their daughters. One of the nicest was a Mademoiselle Davila who is a maid of honour to the Queen, is very pretty and dances beautifully. The maids of honour chaperone themselves and this girl, who is about twenty-four, is made a great deal of and enjoys herself particularly. She took me into the dressing room where I found a good many women sitting about talking to the men who were hanging round the door. Rather to my surprise Davila proceeded to powder herself in front of the glass and then, still more to my surprise, she powdered all the men who were standing in the doorway! Don't be shocked! She is really nice though she is a minx. We stayed till after three, well into the cotillon which I danced with Billy, then we all came home and sat in the drawing room eating sandwiches and talking till four . . ."

Gertrude's parents were shocked at the account of Mademoiselle Davila's doings. That a girl should powder herself at all after leaving her bedroom was questionable, but that she should do it in public and before men was unpardonable. But even under the austere rule of the King, social life among the upper classes in Roumania was more "advanced" than in England. Gertrude records with some surprise meeting a woman at one of the smart parties who had been divorced!

An extract from another letter brings back the light-hearted atmosphere of Bucharest at this time:

". . . Last Sunday which was their first of January, there was a big ball at the palace which was very good fun. I was presented to the King and Queen but the King was so like every other officer that I never could remember who he was and only merciful providence prevented me from giving him a friendly little nod several times during the evening under the impression that he was one of my numerous acquaintance whom I had not yet seen. Billy and I waltzed over his toes once. 'Ware King'—whispered Billy, but it was too late. However he didn't seem to mind. I was taken down to supper by a tall befezed Turk—the Turkish military attaché I think he was. I saw he looked rather depressed and he presently confided to me the cause of his grief; it was very serious; his waistband was too tight and he could not eat any supper! so he stood gloomily by and helped me to all kinds of excellent dishes while I was consumed with a desire to laugh. As for Sztaray, he certainly wears stays. He is the most conceited person I ever met—and I have seen so many here!—he breaks into all conversations with an eternal—'Et moi Madame . . .' The other day at the palace which was rather crowded at first he came up and said to us—'Et moi Madame, c'est évident que je ne danse pas . . .' to which we should have liked to reply that in effect it was quite evident for he was much too tightly laced! . . ."

Bucharest, like Vienna, lived at night. Nothing very much took place before the dinner parties, which started comparatively late, and no one thought of dancing before eleven. The big business men left the routine work to their subordinates and, if there were political crises, the Ministers and diplomatists knew that they would see each other at the parties. Life by the light of day hardly existed. But Gertrude was young, and with that hardy Yorkshire blood in her veins she could do with a few hours sleep and then wanted to be out in the fresh air. No one had thought of out-of-doors entertainments so she set herself to organize them.

It was mid-winter with deep snow everywhere. Gertrude made up sledging expeditions and took the party makers out into the crisp, cold air and brushed away the lethargy of champagne and cigarettes. She decided that some of the men could improve their dancing and that all could afford to learn new steps, so she started a dancing class and taught Bucharestian diplomacy the Boston! Later in the season she suggested tennis as a relaxation and counteractive to overeating, but two difficulties stood in her way, the lack of a proper court and good players. But this did not deter her and in a few weeks she was holding tennis parties, which the young bloods and belles of Bucharest, and many of the older diplomatists, would have no more thought of missing than a court ball!

Before returning to England, Gertrude accompanied her uncle and aunt on a visit to Constantinople. It was her first contact with the Orient and her enthusiasm for all she saw was instantaneous. She seemed to sense the East, she appreciated all the little details, the people had something in common with her, the bazaars with all their colours and smells absorbed her. Her romantic instincts came to the surface and she was closer to Billy Lascelles than at any other time.

A passage from Gertrude's book *Persian Pictures*, published some years later, is a master's etching of Constantinople:

> ". . . From the Scutari hill top the eye is greeted by one of the most enchanting prospects the world has to show—the blue waters of Marmora traversed by greener Bosphorus currents, light mists resting along the foot of the hill-bound coast of Asia, a group of islands floating on the surface of the water, the Golden Horn glimmering away northwards, with the marble walls of the Seraglio stretching a long white finger between it and the sea, Stamboul crowned with minarets and domes. Flocks of gray birds flit aimlessly across the water—the restless souls of women, says Turkish legend—the waves lap round the tower of Leander, the light wind comes whispering down between the exquisite Bosphorus shores, bringing the breath of Russian steppes to shake the plane leaves in Scutari streets. Constantinople the Magnificent gathers her rags round her, throws over

her shoulders her imperial robe of sunshine, and sits in peaceful state with her kingdom of blue waters at her feet . . ."

In many ways this visit to Constantinople and the Balkans was the end of the carefree phase in Gertrude's life. There were many gay periods before her, but somehow that complete light-heartedness and laughter of youth gradually faded into the background. It was as if the grim wastes of Asia had rung out the Fate motif which would inevitably draw her back to the East, never to escape.

CHAPTER IV

Gertrude's return to the formal life of England was a shock. She had spent six months in the careless atmosphere of the smart set in Bucharest where convention was more an expression than a fact and people laughed light-heartedly because they were gay. She came back, just of age, to undergo her first Season under the stern gaze of Victorian matrons and the rigid social codes of an aging Queen.

London society was still governed by the great families which had held sway at Court for generations. The Cavendishes, the Cecils, the Howards, the Stanleys, set the pace which rarely broke out of a majestic walk. It was the age of chaperons, and woe betide any young lady who appeared in public not heavily guarded by an older woman. Even in the routine of daily life a girl could not journey abroad alone. It would be out of the question for Gertrude to go out shopping unaccompanied, she could not visit a picture gallery without a female friend or a maid, and had she strolled down Piccadilly at high noon alone, she would have been for ever stamped as a woman of scant morals.

There were, of course, no reputable night clubs and ladies rarely dined in restaurants. Sitting out too long with one partner at a ball was audibly commented on and Mrs. Bell was shocked when Gertrude confessed that she had driven alone with a man in a hansom from one party to another.

Chaperons were everywhere, and one who would let her charge out of her sight would feel that she had condoned mortal sin. Even when Gertrude and her friends took part in amateur theatricals an old lady sat in the wings. On one of these occasions she fell off the back of the stage and was discovered after the performance unconscious. When she was revived her consternation was almost hysterical at the thought of having remained oblivious, for so long, of the might-have-beens.

Going for a ride in the country was carried out in a cavalcade of suitable escorts, including grooms and family coachmen. The reading of books had a strict censorship, and at the age of twenty-two, after two years at Oxford and a season in Bucharest, Gertrude was reproved for reading Bourget's *Le Disciple.*

Because it was the simplest thing to do, Gertrude conformed, as far as possible, to the conventions of the day, but there were moments when she revolted. She made a trip alone in the underground and one day paid a visit to her friend Mary Talbot, who had emancipated herself and worked in the slums of the East End of London, where maids and chaperons would be out of the question. But her action was regarded as a departure from the normal and people like Miss Talbot were looked upon as eccentrics not to be encouraged.

It was all a form of snobbery, a dying relic of the days when the upper classes had their squires and ladies-in-waiting, which separated them from the common herd which waited on itself. The British are a people of tradition, and while with the accession of Edward VII these conventions were considerably relaxed, young girls did not obtain their freedom from chaperonage until after 1914.

Gertrude was presented at Court, which in those days was called a "drawing room" and took place in the afternoon. She made little comment on the ceremony or on Queen Victoria, but she wrote a detailed description of the dress she wore. She attended dinners at the Duke of Devonshire's and at the "Joe" Chamberlains' and other well-known houses of Victorian London. In addition to the social "pillars" she met interesting people such as the du Mauriers and Anstey and Sidney Webb and the ill-fated Sir Redvers Buller. She went to Ascot where she wagered in a small way, and made the annual pilgrimage to Lord's with her brother for the Eton and Harrow match.

These social activities did not prevent her from keeping up with her studies. She defied convention by investing in a bicycle on which she rode to the British Museum when she wanted to do serious reading.

Extracts from two letters written in 1892 show how easily she could change her mood and adapt herself to different atmospheres:

"We spent a madly amusing five days in Canterbury, of which nothing remains to tell except that we danced every night, saw a good deal of cricket and talked a little. Do you remember discussing what other girls do with their days? Well I have found out—they spend their entire time rushing from house to house for cricket weeks, which means cricket all day and dancing all night; your party consists of the eleven and enough girls to pair off with—you discuss byes and wides and

Kemp at the wicket and Hearn's batting and any other topic of a similar nature, but it's all great fun . . ."

and a few months later she writes:

"I have been reading Latin with great energy. It's a language of which I know very little but whose difficulties must be mastered somehow for I constantly find myself brought up against a blank wall by my ignorance of it . . ."

A young man called Bertie Crackanthorpe paid court to Gertrude at this time, but she was not attracted to him though, with feminine instinct, she kept him dangling for a while before dismissing him. She saw a lot of Billy Lascelles, but the boy and girl romance had faded and he had become a gay companion. Her romances were all in the nature of mild flirtations which did not touch her heart. A lovely, light-hearted girl who did not want her life complicated by temporary affairs. Yet she was moving rapidly towards a crisis in her sentimental life which was not only to alter her whole existence but change the map of Asia. It all came about suddenly and unexpectedly through her aunt of the Bucharest days.

Sir Frank Lascelles had been appointed British Minister to Tehran and in May 1892 Lady Lascelles invited Gertrude to accompany her to Persia. With the joyous memories of Bucharest fresh in her mind, Gertrude accepted and gaily turned her back on the restricting atmosphere of London.

The party, in addition to Lady Lascelles and Gertrude, consisted of her cousin Florence Lascelles, who later became Lady Spring-Rice, and Thorn, Lady Lascelles' maid.

Thorn's future also lay in the Orient, for she eventually married an Englishman out there and settled in Syria where, many years later, Gertrude used to visit her. Mr. Bell and Billy Lascelles travelled as far as Paris and saw the party off on board the Orient Express . . .

The grim notes of the Fate motif which had sounded warningly in Constantinople in 1888 boomed out again as the train carried Gertrude towards Tehran. The untamed Asiatic continent, which captures the minds of Occidentals as the Western Hemisphere never does the Oriental, was waiting to dominate and enslave her.

Had not Gertrude accepted the invitation to go to Persia in 1892, it is to be wondered if the Orient would have completely claimed her and, through the succeeding circumstances, Arabia been invaded by Lawrence and Feisal become the king of Iraq. The sudden twists of destiny which alter people's lives are hard to understand, but if ever there is evidence of a small incident altering history it is Gertrude's journey to Tehran.

For the moment she was deaf to the mutterings of Fate drowned by the clattering of the wheels which bore her across Europe. She had taken Persian lessons before leaving England and, in the intervals of looking out of the carriage window at the ever-changing scenery, she studied her Ollendorff, and was delighted on arriving in Constantinople to find that she could decipher the Arabic characters in the mosques.

Only a few days were spent in Turkey's capital, but Gertrude was up every morning at sunrise visiting and revisiting all the familiar scenes.

She would remain for hours on the Galata Bridge in Constantinople, never weary of watching the people who wandered to and fro, feeling herself one of them. The disdainful walk of the camels, as the stately caravans came in from Tabriz, fascinated her. The sweet, milkless tea, the strong coffee, the rich greasy food, which for many years was to be practically her only diet, were all new to her. The bare, comfortless caravanserais, with their lack of washing and sanitary facilities, were not yet accepted as a matter of course. The huge expanses of treeless country, the rocky hills, the barren soil—settings in which she would make her home for most of the rest of her life—awed her. Every little incident was an adventure, doubly exciting to a girl with a highly developed sense of observation.

Orientals are reputed to be a dignified and impassive people, never allowing outside forces to ruffle them. This characteristic is basically true, but many travellers who have passed through Eastern ports or visited bazaars of the Orient regard the inhabitants as the most excitable in the world. Gertrude encountered the impassive tranquillity of the Persians, she also witnessed their noisy demonstrations of grief and anger and, without hesitation, decided correctly that wailing and beating of breasts at funerals or excitable bargainings in the markets were mere formality. She probably never gave a thought to the rendering of this judgement, but it was greatly through this intuitive understanding of the Oriental mind that she was able to achieve what she did among the peoples of Arabia.

The journey from Constantinople to Tehran was long and tiring. Every method of transportation was used. Trains, ships, carriages, saddle horses. By the time the weary little caravan reached its destination it had been travelling for over a month. Today the same journey takes six days.

From Constantinople, a small and dirty Austrian-Lloyd boat took Lady Lascelles and her charges across the Black Sea to Batoum and on by train to Tiflis and Baku. They were conducted as a special treat to see a "curious phenomenon of nature," the Baku "naphtha wells." Gertrude made a note that the whole country oozed with black, shiny, viscous fluid but it had such a low market value that it was hardly worth collecting. The natives used the oil as fuel for the fires which heated the boilers of their engines because it was cheaper than wood or coal, the highest price being less than a farthing for fifty pounds of naphtha! Thirty years later an international controversy arose over another "naphtha spring," not very far from the one she was now being shown, which caused armies to mobilize and Britain to threaten war. But in 1892 the motor car was not taken seriously and the airplane did not exist. Gertrude could probably have bought the whole of the Baku oil fields for the equivalent of a year's allowance.

The party crossed the Caspian from Baku to Enzelli and drove and rode to Resht, and four days later was in Tehran. After the barren, dusty country which had been crossed during the preceding weeks, Persia's capital looked like the legendary site of the Garden of Eden. The roses were in full bloom and rambled over the Legation buildings, covering them in a mantle of yellow and white and scarlet and purple.

"It's like the 'Beast's' garden," exclaimed Gertrude, "a perfect nightmare of roses!"

And as in the "Beast's" garden of the fairy story, there

was someone who would make Gertrude see the world under a quite different colour.

In her first letter from Persia she tells of the Legation staff, briefly, amusingly but impersonally. Then comes the description of the First Secretary and in a moment she knows all about him and her pen runs on:

> ". . . Mr. Cadogan, tall and red and very thin, agreeable, intelligent, a great tennis player, a great billiard player, an enthusiast about bezique, devoted to riding though he can't ride in the least, smart, clean, well dressed, looking upon us as his special property to be looked after and amused—I like him . . ."

Henry Cadogan, who for the ensuing months was to be Gertrude's constant companion, was the grandson of the third Earl Cadogan and at this time was thirty-three years old.

The impression which he made on Gertrude at that first encounter was reciprocated and from that day on there were no parties, picnics, tennis matches or rides in which the two were not together. Cadogan knew his Persia intimately and understood its problems. He spoke and read the language, and, while furnishing Gertrude with a Persian teacher, it was he who taught her how to learn. He supplied her with the right books to read and explained the difference between Oriental and Occidental idiom. He made her see the Persians in a different light to that usually accepted by people of the West, who regard all coloured men as coolies. Seeing Persia through the understanding eyes of someone she liked made all the difference to Gertrude's stay in the country and influenced her attitude towards Asiatics.

The Persian teacher selected for her by Henry Cadogan

was called Sheik Hassan, a cultured man whose intermediary of conversation with his pupil was indifferent French. He used to ride up to the Legation from Tehran on a mule and, exhausted by his exercise, sink down with a sigh of relief on a carpet beside the cool stream which bubbled through the garden. Gertrude never discovered what Hassan thought about; he had a poor opinion of Persian politics and the Shah, but neither had he much respect for Occidental ways; often he was supremely bored with the lesson and would yawn deeply and at frequent intervals. But his teaching must have been efficient, if one judges by Gertrude's translations of Persian poets and her commentaries on Persian literature. Perhaps it was the enthusiasm of Henry Cadogan, perhaps that persevering character which never gave up anything which it had begun.

For the moment, the learning of Persian was merely a means to appreciate all she saw in Tehran. Everything was new and unexpected and much more exciting than Bucharest and utterly different to London.

Soon after Gertrude's arrival Queen Victoria's birthday was celebrated with all the usual ceremonial ritual. There was a review of the tattered, ill-disciplined army by the Shah, to whom Gertrude was introduced. The Shah was notorious for his off-hand attitude to Europeans, but he was charming to Gertrude due, she found out later, to his awe of her uncle who, when things were not being done according to his lights, had no hesitation in talking frankly to His Majesty. The review, and more especially the Persian army, caused Gertrude endless amusement and she could not resist writing about it in her *Persian Pictures:*

". . . At a street corner a group of soldiers are shaking the branches of a mulberry tree, and eagerly devouring the sickly fruit which falls into the dust at their feet. Judging from the appearance of the Persian army, a foreigner would be tempted to conclude that it subsisted entirely upon white mulberries, and was reduced to a state of starvation when the summer was over. The hands of the paymasters are adhesive in the East; but a small proportion of his earnings reaches the common soldier, and mulberries, flavoured with dust, have at least the merit of furnishing him with an inexpensive meal. His outward man is not calculated to inspire much alarm in the breast of his enemies. His gait is slouching, his uniform torn and discoloured; not infrequently he wears his shirt outside his trousers, and the ragged flounce of brownish grey linen hanging below his tunic lends him an air anything but martial. His temperament seems to be childlike and peaceable in the extreme. He amuses himself while he is on guard with foolish games and it is related that on a certain occasion a person of importance found one of the palace sentries engaged in knitting stockings and the other turning an honest penny by the sale of apples . . ."

After the Shah's review there was a garden party at the British Legation for the foreign diplomatists in Tehran and a few Persians, and a dinner party that night for the British and Persians. Gertrude sat between two Persians, one of whom had been at Oxford and was ultra Occidental, while the other had never left Tehran and had some grievance at being placed next a very young girl and made little attempt to understand Gertrude's Ollendorffian rendering of his language.

This kind of official banquet was rather the exception in Tehran and the life of diplomatists was much more informal than in other capitals.

Gertrude learned the mysteries of hawking and went out

with the falconers to kill quail. She played tennis on a court of beaten mud and made excursions into the mountains on horseback, which led to the discovery that the old-fashioned riding habit was impractical for the kind of expeditions she was undertaking, so she invented a short riding skirt, but did not yet think of riding astride. She shopped in the bazaars and made friends with the merchants and in all she did Henry Cadogan was beside her.

A little more than six weeks after Gertrude's arrival in the Persian capital, the young secretary had become an essential part of her life and she wrote to her step-mother in June of 1892:

> ". . . Mr. Cadogan is the real treasure; it is certainly unexpected and undeserved to have come all the way to Tehran and find someone so delightful at the end. Florence and I like him immensely; he rides with us, he arranges plans for us, he brings his dogs to call on us, he plays with our kittens, he shows us lovely things from the bazaars, he is always there when we want him and never when we don't . . ."

and a little later:

> ". . . I spent the rest of the afternoon in a long and interesting talk with Mr. Cadogan who is a real joy to talk to and charming besides; we rode back through the dusk and reached home just in time for dinner . . ."

As the temperature rose with the beginning of the hot weather the foreign Legations moved to Gulahek, their summer quarters in the hills. Cholera was stalking through the bazaars of Persia and it was safer for the diplomatists to be away in the cool of the uplands. Here life was much more informal than in Tehran. The Legation was small and intimate and meals were taken out of doors or under a huge tent. But the place appealed to Gertrude even more than the capital and she wrote to Horace Marshall:

"... in this country the men wear flowing robes of green and white and brown, the women lift the veil of a Raphael Madonna to look at you as they pass; wherever there is water a luxuriant vegetation springs up and where there is not there is nothing but stone and desert. Oh the desert round Tehran! miles and miles of it with nothing, *nothing* growing; ringed in with bleak bare mountains snow-crowned and furrowed with the deep courses of torrents. I never knew what desert was till I came here; it is a very wonderful thing to see; and suddenly in the middle of it all, out of nothing, out of a little cold water, springs up a garden. Such a garden! trees, fountains, tanks, roses and a house in it, the houses which we heard of in fairy tales when we were little: inlaid with tiny slabs of looking-glass in lovely patterns, blue tiled, carpeted, echoing with the sound of running water and fountains. Here sits the enchanted prince, solemn, dignified, clothed in long robes. He comes down to meet you as you enter, his house is yours, his garden is yours, better still his tea and fruit are yours ...

"Ah we have no hospitality in the west and no manners. I felt ashamed almost before the beggars in the street—they wear their rags with a better grace than I my most becoming habit and the veils of the commonest women are far better put on than mine ...

"What else can I give you but fleeting impressions caught and hardened out of all knowing? I can tell you of a Persian merchant in whose garden, stretching all up the mountain side, we spent a long day, from dawn to sunset, breakfasting, lunching, teaing on nothing but Persian foods. He is noted for his hospitality; every evening parties of friends arrive unexpectedly, 'he goes out, entertains them,' said the Persian who told me about it, 'spreads a banquet before them and relates to them stories half through the night. Then cushions are brought and carpeted mattresses and they lie down in one of the guest houses in the garden and sleep till dawn when they rise and repair to the bath in the village.'

"Isn't it charmingly like the Arabian Nights! but that is the charm of it all and it has none of it changed; every day I meet our aged kalendars and ladies who I am sure have suits of swans feathers laid up in a chest at home, and some time when I open a new jar of rose water I know that instead of a sweet smell, the great smoke of one of Suleiman's afreets will come out of its neck . . ."

At first the cholera was satisfied with taking its toll of dead in the eastern boundaries of the country but, as the summer drew on, it moved rapidly westwards. The Persians, with their Oriental fatalism, took no precautions and made no preparations to meet the scourge; they would not admit that the cholera could touch Tehran and continued to drink bad water and eat over-ripe fruit. When the first case appeared in the capital, there was panic. The doctors shut up their stores and made for the open country, the landlords turned their tenants into the streets at the first symptoms of the disease, women and children were cast out of the harems, few even had the courage to bury their dead. Those who could afford it took to the desert and camped on the barren plains or, if they were lucky, beside streams, but the cholera followed them and polluted the water, and those in flight fell by the wayside. The Shah was making a tour through his kingdom when the disease appeared. He at once gave orders that this scourge of God must not be allowed to enter his camp and hurried away into the mountains, but the cholera pursued him and fifty of his retinue died without his being informed. The only people who remained at their posts, disregarding the dangers of death and doing all they could to alleviate the suffering, were the American missionaries, a devoted band of heroes who fought the relentless plague until it disappeared as suddenly as it had come.

The members of the Legation staffs were spared though many of the servants died and it was a trying, anxious time with death decimating villages all around their summer quarters.

Gertrude's attitude towards the cholera was curiously aloof. There was no fear for herself and a kind of detached attitude of an observer noting the reactions of those about her. More especially did she watch Henry Cadogan, but he took the epidemic and the deaths and the Persians fleeing in panic all as a matter of course and laughed at the thought of being caught himself. Nothing could have brought him closer to Gertrude who had not discovered the meaning of the word fear, and was rapidly finding out the significance of the word love.

Eager to have someone near and dear explain this state of mind, she begged her father to visit her. She suggested that they make a journey on horseback through Persia to Bushire, Isfahan and Shiraz. Mr. Bell would have liked to come, but his departure was delayed by political events in England. After six years out of office, Mr. Gladstone's party was in power for the last time. Mr. Bell, who had always been a firm believer in Gladstonian policy, found that his allegiance was not proof against the Government's determination to bring in Home Rule for Ireland. He accordingly stood for the Middlesborough constituency as a Liberal Unionist, but he was defeated.

In the meanwhile, Gertrude was restless. She had pangs of homesickness, moments of unexplainable depression and recurring insomnia, all symptoms of that painful ailment of the heart which medicines cannot cure. She tried to occupy herself by organizing diplomatic tennis tournaments on a bumpy court; cricket was started with ancient balls and still more ancient bats and puzzled the foreign attachés by its complicated rules. There was a race meeting at which Gertrude won thirty shillings. Some of the races were of the orthodox breed with members of the *corps diplomatique* acting as jockeys, but the majority were Persian contests with Persian riders dressed in the most astonishing colours. Some of these latter races were five miles long and it was not unusual for the winning horse to die after passing the winning post!

These pastimes kept the diplomatists and their attendants occupied and made them forget the cholera. They also brought Gertrude and Henry Cadogan into daily and close contact and it was clear to the most junior clerk that a disease infinitely more relentless than the plague had made its appearance in the Legation summer camp.

One evening Gertrude and Henry sat in the deserted garden of some nobleman of long ago. Fountains played among the tall, black cypress trees, pink briar roses spread themselves in all directions and every little rivulet of bubbling water was fringed with scented violets. They were both very still as they sat close in the deepening twilight. A Persian in a long robe came out of a pavilion carrying a musical instrument and, seating himself beside a fountain, began to play. The darkness increased and one by one the stars flashed red in the sky. The Persian musician was no longer visible, but he played on, while the breeze caressed the two with rose-scented kisses and the nightingales called from the trees. It was a setting for Scheherazade, the peace of the Garden of Eden. Few words were spoken, but when the lovers parted they shared their secret.

With the morning, Gertrude had to temporarily forget romance and be practical. In spite of being in Persia, in spite of the cholera and the fact that she was in love, she had been brought up to respect the social codes of Victorian England, and, before all, she must ask her parents' consent to an engagement. She had, up to that date, never referred to Cadogan except formally with the prefix of Mister and it would not have occurred to her to consider herself officially engaged or in any way preparing for marriage without the approval of her father and step-mother.

She wrote a long letter, simple and straight to the point, and then had to wait for the reply. It was a long, straining wait and with no certainty of an approving answer. Henry Cadogan had charm and ability and undoubtedly a fine future in the diplomatic service; but he was a younger son whose career had not been unchequered, and he had little private income. Gertrude would have a dowry, but in those days a young man who wished to marry had to show the parents of the prospective bride that he had enough to keep her "in the way to which she was accustomed."

So the lovers waited, letting their idyl take its course. They rode together, they took long walks and vied with each other in catching trout, using local flies tied by a Persian nobleman and more attractive to fish than the elaborate March Browns from Hardy's. They played backgammon in the garden of a poetic-minded merchant and failed to defeat him. Sometimes they used to day-dream and see themselves riding out over the desert from Tehran. They would form a caravan and travel the length and breadth of Persia and Mesopotamia and Arabia, exploring, excavating, studying the tribal customs and languages. Henry would become the great authority on the East and would be sent out by the British Government to teach the warring tribes to live in harmony. Gertrude would be his companion, smoothing out difficulties through tact and friendliness while her husband took care of Her Majesty's Dominions.

In their imagination they saw the difficulties with which they would have to contend, the obstacles which they would have to surmount, the growing importance of their work and the eventual crowning with success of their insuperable determination to succeed.

It seemed impossible to imagine that anything would intervene to alter these plans, so solid were the foundations which they were mentally laying down. . . .

They were taken to see the treasure house of the Shah. It was an amazing place in which swords and cups and carpets studded with jewels, and golden boxes full of precious stones were thrown together with glass cases crammed with quack remedies, and toothbrushes, in priceless cloisonné bowls, which the Shah had collected during his travels abroad.

They discussed politics and differed, although Gertrude tried to bring Cadogan round to her way of regarding the Home Rule question. They talked about their future rather despondently, wondering how long it would be before Henry was earning a large enough salary to marry, while Gertrude showed apprehension at the prospect of having to spend most of her life outside England! They had little quarrels, followed by terrific remorses when Gertrude sent Henry to bed without a last good night.

On September 14th the fatal letter arrived. Gertrude read it, torn by conflicting emotions. While her parents wrote sympathetically and lovingly, the engagement was not encouraged. No definite reasons were given for the lack of enthusiasm, but it was suggested that Gertrude should come home and find out whether the glamour of Persian rose gardens had not had something to do with her romantic mood.

A few years later she would have probably dismissed her parents' objections gently but firmly, but, although past twenty-four years of age, she could not forget the traditions of the times to which she belonged. She wrote a dutiful reply to her step-mother and, while not by any means suggesting that she would give up Henry Cadogan, she agreed to an immediate return to England. Her letter reads:

"Yesterday we sat in the Movara garden and discussed it [her parents' letter] in all its bearings, we felt we could not go on pretending to each other any more when things looked so black for us . . . We talked much of you; I had given him several of your letters to read for I wanted him so much to know you, and he does know a little from them and from me how dear and how beloved you are. 'Perhaps when you go home she will write once to me,' he said—which sounded so pathetic and made my own unhappiness seem so endlessly selfish, for I have you for help and for consolation when I go home and he has nobody and nothing in front of him but more years of this weary place. He was devoted to his own mother who died a few years ago—if only she had been alive she would have known how to help, as you will know. The thing I can bear least is that you or Papa should ever think anything of him which is not noble and gentle and good. That is all of him I have ever known, I wish I could pass on my impression to you untouched and unspoiled, the side of him he has shown a woman when he loved her—do you remember Browning? He quoted that to me once long ago and I wondered vaguely if it were more than form of words. Everything I think and write brings us back to things we have spoken of together, sentences of his that come flashing like sharp swords; you see for the last three months nothing I have done or thought has not had him in it, the essence of it all.

"It is very horrid of me to write like this, it will only make you sorry quite uselessly and needlessly. You must not think for a moment that if I could choose I would not have it all over again, impatience and pain and the going which is yet to come. It is worth it all, more than worth it. Some people live all their lives and never have this wonderful thing; at least I have known it and have seen life's possibilities suddenly open in front of me —only one may cry just a little when one has to turn away and take up the old narrow life again; I am so foolishly hopeful, not because I see any good way through our difficulties, but only because it is so impossible to believe that one cannot have the one big thing one wants more than life when one has had all the little things one really didn't care much about . . . Oh Mother, Mother . . ."

Gertrude spent her last days in Persia with Henry, going over and over the problems of their future. He was tender and sympathetic as Gertrude assured him that nothing could separate them, but they parted with a kind of helpless, hopeless feeling which neither of them was able to explain. Gerald Lascelles escorted his cousin on the return journey which was just as long and tiring and without the joyous anticipation of the outward trip. Gertrude showed no outward emotion but every turn of the wheels which took her further from Henry seemed to bruise her heart.

As the ship set out across the Black Sea, she remained on deck watching the receding Asiatic coast which gradually faded in the mist. Her mind was filled with evil forebodings and she felt inclined to beg the captain to turn back and let her remain in the country where she had found real happiness . . .

It was cold and wintry when the two travellers at last reached London. Mr. Bell had come down from Yorkshire to meet his daughter and comforted her as best he could while she sobbed out her heart to him. She soon went north to her home and tried to explain all she felt to her step-mother.

The parents were baffled. This was not the passing fancy of a young girl but the grief of a woman desperately in love. It was the first love of her life and the tone of her voice and the look in her eyes made them realize that it would be the last. Gertrude swept aside every objection to her marriage with Henry Cadogan, until her father consented. The black clouds of despondency melted under a sunshine of happiness, the world seemed once more to be at Gertrude's feet, but she had forgotten that there were other things in the Orient to contend with besides parents' consents . . .

* * *

Gertrude never saw Henry Cadogan again. During the summer of 1893 the cholera stretched out its stinking hands and struck down the young diplomatist. After a few days' illness he died almost exactly on the anniversary of his becoming engaged to Gertrude.

PART II

WOMANHOOD

CHAPTER V

THE DEATH OF HENRY CADOGAN closed a chapter in the life of Gertrude Bell and opened a new one in international history.

Had Henry lived, Gertrude would undoubtedly have married him and become the wife of a British diplomatist with a more or less conventional life. She would have probably done much to further his career, but it is unusual for British Civil Servants to find the opportunity to do anything particularly outstanding. At the best, Henry Cadogan might have retired in his sixties after two, possibly three, ambassadorial posts.

The change of orientation which the death of her fiancé brought about in Gertrude was literal, for it was due to his influence that her mind and her thoughts turned towards Asia.

The East had attracted Gertrude when she first set foot in Constantinople in 1889, it had fascinated her when she travelled to Persia in 1892, but there was something more than the interest which any intelligent person feels for new countries, especially in the days when journeys were complicated affairs. It was Henry Cadogan who had made her feel the charm of the East. It was he who had helped her to learn Persian and understand the literature of the country. It was he who had developed her sympathy for Oriental peoples and made her appreciate their problems. Gertrude did not perhaps realize how deeply Persia and the desert had become part of her until her fiancé's death. When it was all over and her grief had subsided, she not only knew to what extent the East had captured her imagination but regarded it as part of something which she could never have. Her journeys, her explorations, her excavations in the Orient, her eventual administrative posts, became the only interests in her life and they were woven into the memory of her great love. Henry Cadogan had found something unexplainable in Persia and had died in the country without the solution. Gertrude set out to solve the problem and she too died among those people of Asia, whom Cadogan had loved, but with the problem solved. In all that follows in Gertrude's unparalleled career in Western Asia, the underlying motif and incentive cannot be discounted.

For some months after Henry's death, Gertrude's happy nature faded and she remained alone in her home, grieving. The realization that none of their day-dreams would materialize, that Henry was gone and she could never recapture those glorious times again, was almost too much for her to stand. She had hidden her great hurt as best she could from her parents and friends, but there were moments when she revolted against the Victorian standards which made it necessary for a grown woman to mould her life on a family's wishes. She brooded over the might-have-beens, living over and over again those brief moments of happiness.

Then, one day, the reaction came. She calmed herself

and tried to think sensibly. As there could be no turning back, she must go forward and go forward alone, but not to that old life of teas and dinners and aimless travels—she had to have an interest, a supreme objective . . . then the idea came . . .

Why not do the things which she and Henry had planned in the gardens of Tehran and by the streams of Gulahek? Why not go back to the East, take the caravan, explore, excavate, try to fulfil the mission which Henry Cadogan had set for them both— Alone? New life welled up in Gertrude as these thoughts took shape and she discovered that, while her lover could not be with her physically, in spirit he would be near her in all these ventures.

Thus gradually her buoyant courage asserted itself and she realized that she had things to do.

Perhaps what helped her most in this crisis was her affection for her father. It was more than the usual instinctive love of a daughter, and amounted to an almost blind adoration. While at Queen's College and at Oxford, she wrote letters which were exclusively for her father's ear and after the tragedy of Henry Cadogan she drew him even closer. She consulted him on the smallest details of her daily life as well as on problems encountered in her work. She wanted him beside her during the long periods she was away from home:

". . . I can't help feeling a dreadful tightening at the heart at the thought of not seeing you within measurable time," she writes. "I do sometimes want you so much that I can scarcely bear it . . ."

". . . Your most beloved letter of November 26th—I was glad

to have it—it made me feel quite warm inside. I'm perfectly aware that I don't merit so much love, but the nicest thing about love is that you can have it without merit . . ."

First of all tempted to return to Tehran, Gertrude saw that this would only reopen the wound, and during the next five years she travelled all over Europe and once round the world, concentrating her energies on writing.

As an immediate result of this first visit to the Orient, a book entitled *Persian Pictures* was published. In it the life of the town and the bazaars, the rose-scented gardens and the desolate places so near to them, the nomads, the merchants and the noble Persians, are described with a deft touch which makes the reader feel the atmosphere of the country and see its people. To those who know the inside story of Gertrude's life it is easy to sense a sad young heart finding expression in these pages. The book is written as personal impressions, but "we" is invariably used. In every line there is the feeling of two people very dear to each other sharing all the loveliness of old Persia.

Gertrude did not want these intimate thoughts to be given to the public and for some time opposed any idea of publication of the book. When finally she yielded to the pressure of her parents, who felt that it was unfair to keep a beautiful piece of literature hidden away, the book was brought out anonymously and it was not until much later that it was re-published under her name. The volume is still in circulation and gives no feeling of being "dated." This is sufficient comment on its merit and there is little doubt that had Gertrude decided to concentrate her energies on writing of this kind she would have held her place with Burton or Fitzgerald.

She eventually published a number of volumes of prose and poetry; [1] and whether she was deliberately writing verse or describing what she saw, in her letters and travel books she maintains a rhythm which is uncannily Oriental without being stilted or forced.

In our book sufficient passages of Gertrude's prose have been quoted to illustrate her craft in this branch of literature and the following are taken at random from her adaptations of Persian poetry:

I cease not from desire till my desire
Is satisfied; or let my mouth attain
My love's red mouth, or let my soul expire,
Sighed from those lips that sought their lips in vain.
Others may find another love as fair;
Upon her threshold I have laid my head
The dust shall cover me, still lying there,
When from my body life and love have fled.

Each curling lock of thy luxuriant hair
Breaks into barbed hooks to catch my heart,
My broken heart is wounded everywhere
With countless wounds from which the red drops start.
Yet when sad lovers meet and tell their sighs,
Not without praise shall Hafiz' name be said,
Not without tears, in those pale companies
Where joy has been forgot and hope has fled.

* * *

The nightingale with drops of his heart's blood
Had nourished the red rose, then came the wind,
And catching at the boughs in envious mood,

[1] Books by Gertrude Bell: *Persian Pictures; Safar Nameh; Poems from the Divan of Hafiz; The Desert and the Sown; The Thousand and One Churches; Amurath to Amurath; The Palace and Mosque of Ukkaidir; Review of the Civil Administration of Mesopotamia.*

A hundred thorns about his heart entwined,
Like to the parrot crunching sugar, good
Seemed the world to me who could not stay
The wind of Death that swept my hopes away.

Light of mine eyes and harvest of my heart,
And mine at least in changeless memory!
Ah! when he found it easy to depart
He left the harder pilgrimage to me!
Oh Camel driver, though the cordage start,
For God's sake help me lift my fallen load,
And Pity be my comrade of the road!

* * *

Wind from the east, oh Lapwing of the day,
I send thee to my Lady, though the way
Is far to Saba, where I bid thee fly;
Lest in the dust thy tameless wings should lie,
Broken with grief, I send thee to thy nest
Fidelity.

* * *

The days of Spring are here! the eglantine,
The rose, the tulip from the dust have risen—
And thou, why liest thou beneath the dust?
Like the full clouds of Spring, these eyes of mine
Shall scatter tears upon the grave thy prison,
Till thou too from the earth thine head shalt thrust.

* * *

But while Gertrude made no attempt to revisit the scenes of her great happiness, her mind was set on the East and she continued her studies of Persian and began to learn Arabic. She employed native teachers in London and by 1896 had read the Koran and much of the *Arabian Nights* in their original tongues. But again, as at Oxford, that mixture of youthful enthusiasm for life and study remained. In a letter from London she talks enthusiastically about a fancy dress ball and the costume she wore and then of spending the morning at the British Museum "reading the life of Hafiz with a Latin crib!"

She went to Italy and lived for some time in Venice where her first step was to learn Italian. She was there in April of 1896 for the arrival of the Kaiser on board his great white yacht *The Hohenzollern.* Venice was decked with banners and flags; as in the days of the Doges salutes were fired, and King Humbert and Queen Margherita went on board the yacht to greet William II and take him on shore. This ceremony was actually the public confirmation of the Triple Alliance which was to cause so much trouble in 1914, and in a letter to her father, commenting on this event, she cryptically remarks:

> "I only wish it had not been that particular emperor we were welcoming!"

She was, however, to come into much closer contact with William II as, in 1897, she once more went to stay with her aunt who was now British Ambassadress in Berlin.

A curious kaleidoscope these visits to Lady Lascelles. Inconsequent Bucharest society, a tragic queen; romance in Persian rose gardens; and now the stiff formality of that imperial autocrat whose unhealthy mind was soon to throw the world into chaos.

But even the humourless magnificence of the megalomaniac Emperor did not quench Gertrude's sense of humour. On January 22 she was presented at the German Court and ends an account of her nervousness during the ordeal with:

"... the 'Allerhöchst' looked extremely well in a red uniform —I couldn't look at the empress much as I was busy avoiding Aunt Mary's train. She presented me and then stood aside while I made two curtsies. Then I wondered what the dickens to do next, but Aunt Mary made a little sign, so I 'enjambéd' her train and fled ..."

She skated at Potsdam and was eventually brought into personal contact with the Emperor and Empress at a State performance of Shakespeare's *Henry IV*.

The procedure was rigid and pompous. Chaperoned by a lady-in-waiting, Gertrude and her cousin Florence were taken to the theatre and sat in the second row of chairs, for, although the Imperial party was in a box, no one, not of blood royal, could sit in the front row. During the interval the two English girls were sent for by the Kaiser and found him in an anteroom behind his box drinking tea with the Empress. Gertrude thought the Empress stiff and alarming but the Emperor eager to make her feel at ease. An impression of twitching nerves, talking all the time without waiting for answers. He told Gertrude that Shakespeare's plays were never properly acted in England and it was only the Germans who really studied or understood Shakespeare. Gertrude, with her usual directness, was about to challenge this statement when, luckily for her, a chair, on which one of the courtiers was sitting, collapsed under him and broke up the interview.

She attended two Court Balls, at one of which Florence Lascelles danced the gavotte before their majesties, but the whole atmosphere was too artificial for Gertrude's temperament and her instinctive dislike of the Kaiser continued. She could not take the man seriously and his nervous mannerisms seemed to dominate the magnificent setting in which he lived. At one of the Court functions she met the ill-fated Archduke whose assassination was to precipitate the world war of 1914, but her mind only recorded a plain individual in a gorgeous uniform. A ball at the British Embassy she enjoyed, but she felt none of those waves of carefree enjoyment of the gay parties in Bucharest or the informal gatherings in Tehran with Henry Cadogan to laugh with when the guests had left. This visit had a note of hidden tragedy as it was the last time that Gertrude was to see her aunt. Lady Lascelles died on April 3, 1897, leaving an irreparable blank in Gertrude's life.

Almost immediately after her return from Germany, Gertrude started on a trip round the world with her brother Maurice which was to take them six months.

Oddly enough, this first long journey did not make much impression on her. That is to say the life on board ship, the passengers, the games, the sea itself, entertained her, but the ports of call were of no more importance than railway stations during a train journey. Gertrude had to become closely acquainted with peoples to comment on them, and if she could not take part in their lives, speak their language and see through their eyes it was waste of time thinking about them.

The travelled attitude of the tourist, who takes a round-the-world cruise and comes back laden with photographs and cheap curios from the ports where his luxury ship has called, was not Gertrude's. At the time of her death, she had visited most of the countries of the world but she would only admit to knowing a small area between the River Tigris and the Red Sea.

The moment she returned to London, she set to work again with her professors of Arabic and Persian. She had made no plans, but her desire to go back to the East was taking definite shape. Before making the final move, however, she travelled to Greece with her father, where she encountered Doctor Hogarth, the famous archaeologist, and the brother of her Oxford friend, Janet. Doctor Hogarth was, at the time, excavating the six-thousand-year-old city of Melos. Gertrude's flair for archaeology, a flair which she had already shown at the age of seventeen when examining Roman tombs with her brother at Rochester, at once made itself evident, and for the next few days she remained at Melos absorbed in Hogarth's work while he was delighted to find someone so charming and so intelligent.

Gertrude's last venture, before she set out to begin her travels in the Orient, was in Switzerland, and gives the first glimpse of the fearless spirit of adventure which the feminine and attractive exterior concealed.

Ever since she had climbed trees as a child and Devonshire cliffs as a young girl, she had been interested in mountaineering and had done a good deal of this in Switzerland. In August of 1899 she decided to climb the Grand Pic de la Meije in the Dauphiné, a peak only attempted by the most experienced Alpinists. Gertrude had not this experience, but she undertook the ascent of that rocky crag, the crossing of the glacier and its treacherous crevasses, with the same unconcern as she would have played a set of tennis. Every kind of contretemps presented itself during the scaling of the mountain, but she reached the summit and got down again, in spite of a blizzard which kept her and her guides clinging to a precipice for some hours.

This adventure in the Dauphiné was the closing scene of what might be called the normal section of Gertrude's life. She was just thirty-one, at an age when most girls would decide that it was time to marry and settle down to the formal life of England. She had loved and, through no fault of her own, had lost, she had travelled and studied, she had met most of the contemporary distinguished people of her time and there seemed enough to make looking back a sufficient satisfaction that her life had not been wasted. And yet Gertrude was still on the threshold of real achievements, and during the course of the next twenty-six years was to make for herself the name which would rank with Clive and Stanley and Lawrence of Arabia.

CHAPTER VI

THE DESERT HAD FLIRTED WITH GERTRUDE when she met it for the first time during her visit to Persia in 1892. It had flirted with her enough to arouse her curiosity and remain in her thoughts for seven years. When she saw it again in the winter of 1899, she knew it once more as the intriguing and unknown quantity of the lover who comes into the life of a young girl and flits out again without any physical contact. For a while she continued the flirtation, amused at combating the inevitable, and then happily abandoned herself to the relentless embrace.

The hold which the desert puts on people is as hard to explain as the attraction of man for woman. To some it is a hideous, cruel wilderness to be avoided and feared; to others a dominating, charming suitor who conquers by very force of character. The blinking expanses of stones and scrub, the orange sunsets, the burning days and the icy nights, capture something in certain hearts as indefinable as love. Its soft beauty, as the twilight begins or the moon rises, makes people forget the scorching winds and the sand storm, and the human being who has once felt the charm of the desert will never forget it and will be under its spell for the rest of his life.

There are old officers of the Sahara camel corps, whose one thought during their service has been retirement in some rural French village, but after a year or so of this peaceful existence in a temperate climate they have gone back to the desert to end their days in its haunting arid wastes.

Gertrude had these feelings from the very beginning of her contact with the desert and wrote in her book *The Desert and the Sown:*

> "I looked out into the night and saw the desert no longer empty, but set thicker with human associations than any city. Every little line of it took on significance, every stone was like the ghost of a hearth in which the warmth of Arab life was hardly cold, though the fire might have been extinguished this hundred years. It was a city of shadowy outlines, visible one under the other, fleeting and changing, combining into new shapes elements that are as old as time, the new indistinguishable from the old and the old from the new.
>
> "There is no name for it. The Arabs do not speak of the desert or wilderness as we do. Why should they? To them it is neither desert nor wilderness, but a land of which they know every feature, a mother country whose smallest product has a use sufficient for their needs. They know, or at least they knew in the days when their thoughts shaped themselves in deathless verse, how to rejoice in the great spaces and how to honour the rush of the storm . . . They had watched, as they crossed the barren watercourses, the laggard wonders of the night, when the stars seemed chained to the sky as though the dawn would never come . . ."

Gertrude returned to those barren countries of the East because she could not help it, and by the time she had been there a few weeks she knew that nothing would take her away for any length of time. There is no other explanation to give, no ulterior motive to explain why she practically exiled herself in those desolate countries for the greater part of her life. The desert and its people, which she had learned to appreciate with Henry Cadogan, had captured her mind to the exclusion of everything else.

She made her headquarters first of all in Jerusalem and settled down to perfect her Arabic. She had no intention at this time to explore the Arabian peninsula and her first trips were no more than excursions into the neighbourhood. Nevertheless, she had completely detached herself from her home life, and with the exception of a few references in letters to her brother Maurice, who was fighting the Boers in South Africa, all her interests were centred in Arabia. This was an exceptional characteristic in an Englishwoman; for, whereas the male Briton either stays at home for life or else expatriates himself completely to settle in some distant part of the Empire, the female always wishes to get home. There are few so fundamentally unhappy women as the wives of officers in the Indian Army or of planters in the Malay States.

Gertrude never showed the slightest desire to return to live in Yorkshire, and while keeping in touch with her family she rapidly assimilated herself to Arabia. She did not, like Lady Hester Stanhope, by any means "go native," and up to her death wore the most orthodox of Occidental clothes and insisted on her "tea" as if she were at home. What she did do, which is not at all British, was to see and think like the natives with whom she lived without ever letting them feel that she belonged to a dominant race. It was this ability which gained her the inhabitants' affection and enabled her later to do so much for Great Britain in the Near East.

Again writing in *The Desert and the Sown*, she says:

"And for this reason he [the Occidental] will be wiser if he does not seek to ingratiate himself with Orientals by trying to ape their habits, unless he is so skilful that he can pass as one of themselves. Let him treat the laws of others respectfully, but he himself will meet with a far greater respect if he adheres strictly to his own. For a woman this rule is of first importance, since a woman can never disguise herself effectually. That she should be known to come of a great and honoured stock, whose customs are inviolable, is her best claim to consideration."

Another quality which helped Gertrude to feel so happy in this life, so remote from her upbringing, was a sense of humour and an ability to see the comic side of Oriental life. What the Occidental, and especially the Briton and the American, will not take into consideration when dealing with the people of the East, is that their mentality, actions and ways of thinking are almost exactly opposite to Western conception. Even speech in the East is not used for the same purpose as in the West.

If an Arab is asked to dine or make an appointment, he will not answer "Yes" or "No," but "Inschallah," which means "If God wills it." In other words, he will not tempt Destiny, and if Allah does intervene he will not keep the appointment or make any excuse about it. This apparently casual attitude infuriates the Occidental until he realizes that irritation only amuses the Arab as a demonstration of human frailty. There were times at the beginning of Gertrude's career among the people of Western Asia when she used to give way to exasperation, but controlled her irritation when she understood that it led her nowhere. A sense of the absurd and a sense of humour, she decided, carried her much farther than any kind of blustering superiority.

During her wanderings she kept a record of all sorts of queer and amusing conversations.

Gertrude is riding with two Bedouin guides. She is bored with her own thoughts and starts a conversation by asking one of the men called Yunis if he ever goes to Aleppo. "Oh, yes," replies Yunis. He always goes there when his sons are in prison. Gertrude quickly edges away from delicate ground and inquires how many sons Yunis has. Eight, each of his wives has borne him four sons and two daughters, but his second wife cost him a great deal of money. In fact she caused him much trouble as he took her forcibly from her husband and had not only to compensate him but to pay a heavy fine to the judge.

Gertrude, eager to hear of the woman's reactions, asked if she liked this mercenary transaction.

"Without doubt," replied Yunis, "it was her wish."

Inquiring about ruined cities of an old man supplied as a guide:

GERTRUDE: What should I ride out and see?
OLD MAN: Many churches there are, a very great many.
GERTRUDE: Where?
OLD MAN (waving his arm vaguely towards the mountains): Over there, that side.
GERTRUDE: What is the name?
OLD MAN: Ali.
GERTRUDE: No, not your name, the church's name.
OLD MAN: Chandlik.
GERTRUDE: Aren't there any in other directions?
OLD MAN: Not any at all.
A BYSTANDER: Many, a great many, over there there is one.

GERTRUDE: What is the name?
OLD MAN: Ali.
GERTRUDE: Not your name, the church's . . .

And so on and so on.

Conversation with the cook:

GERTRUDE: Oh, Fattuh, to whom does this polar garden belong?
FATTUH: To a priest, lady.
GERTRUDE: Doesn't he mind our camping in it?
FATTUH: He didn't say anything.
GERTRUDE: Did you ask him?
FATTUH: No, my lady.
GERTRUDE: We must give him some bakhshish.
FATTUH: At your Excellency's command. (A pause.) My lady . . .
GERTRUDE: Yes?
FATTUH: The priest is dead.
GERTRUDE: Then I don't think we need bother about the bakhshish.
FATTUH: No, my lady.

At breakfast the cook has made some excellent little mutton sausages.

GERTRUDE (wishing to improve her Arabic): Oh, Fattuh, what is the name of these?
FATTUH: Effendim, these? Their name is sossiglio.

And discussing life's problems with a venerable Kadi:

" 'In Europe,' said the Kadi, 'I have heard that men of science are your prophets.'

" 'And they make answer that they know nothing,' I observed. 'Their eyes have explored the stars, yet they cannot tell us the meaning of the word infinity.'

" 'If you talk of the infinite sky,' remarked the Kadi, 'we know that it is occupied by seven heavens.'

" 'And what beyond the seventh heaven?'

" 'Does not your Excellency know that the number one is the beginning of all things?' said he. 'When you have told me what comes before the number one, I will tell you what lies beyond the seventh heaven!'

"The Pasha laughed and said that if the Kadi had finished his argument he would like to ask me what was the current opinion in Europe in the matter of thought reading.

" 'For,' said he, 'a month ago a ring of price was stolen in my house and I could not find the thief. Now a certain Effendi among my friends hearing of my case, came to me and said:

" ' "I know a man in the Lebanon, skilful in these things!" I said, "Do me the kindness to send for him." And the man came and he sought in Homs, until he found a woman gifted with second sight and he worked spells on her until she spoke and said:

" ' "The thief is so and so and he has taken the ring to his house."

" 'And we sought in the house and found the jewel. This is my experience for the event happened under my eyes.'

"I replied that thought readers in the Lebanon made better use of their gifts than any I had heard of in London and the Pasha said meditatively:

" 'It may be that the woman of the bazaar had a complaint against the man in whose house we found the ring. God alone knows, may His name be exalted!'

"And so we left it."

It is pure Arabian Night and as Gertrude listened to these men she could feel Shah Zaman and King Shahryyar coming to life, with the slaves and the princes and the lovely Scheherazade and Dunyazad, in the same setting where she now found herself. She saw and felt as they did and by this understanding discovered the secret to success among the people of Arabia.

The Arab belongs to a proud and ancient race with traditions dating back long before Mohammed. He has never really been defeated by any nation of the Occident and has himself invaded and occupied half Europe. He does not behave in a superior manner to Europeans and he resents any superior attitude on their part. If then someone from a land which he knows to be the head of a great empire comes and lives with him, shares his food and his hardships and, above all, joins in his conversation on an equal footing, he at once loses all his reserve and there is nothing he will not do to show his appreciation. Neither can this intimacy be acquired by a mere wish to do so. The Arab has to *feel* that he is liked.

Gertrude liked the Arabs and they liked her, the rest was just a matter of letting things take their course.

Gertrude's first expeditions covered the beaten track round about Jerusalem until, feeling safer with her Arabic, she determined to penetrate into the interior of the country and set off in March of 1900 with her own caravan.

Compared with her journeys to come, this one was "tame." Nevertheless, for a woman alone, with an imperfect knowledge of the language and none of the country, it must be regarded as an adventure.

Having bought a horse and engaged a cook, Gertrude set out from Jerusalem at the beginning of March. Her caravan consisted of saddle horses, and donkeys to carry the tents and the provisions. Riding was second nature to her, but she had always used a side saddle and worn a habit. The days were still a long way off when women would don the breeches of men and Gertrude compromised by having a divided skirt made which enabled her to ride astride.

As she moved away from the main roads, she fell in with

other travellers, traders and nomads and pilgrims, and continued with them as far as they went. She talked and joked with them, shared their meals and gained their confidence. The eating of Arab food, squatting on the ground, seemed to come as natural to her as dining at home and she never felt the least afraid of these men, many of whom were outlaws. Her summing-up of these desert people, based partly on instinct and partly on observation, was more accurate than either Burton or Doughty.

"... The nomads," she wrote, "can no more give you a sense of companionship than the wild goats; they are equally unconscious of the desolation which surrounds them—even if you fall into speech with one of them, there are few common topics on which you can converse. He will question you as to your nationality. You try to explain that you are English and come from far across the seas; and he listens attentively, though you know your words throw no light on his boundless ignorance ..."

"Boundless ignorance" precisely explains the nomad. He has no education, does not want any and expects nothing of the world beyond enough to eat and a few rags to cover his body. Story books and motion pictures have created a kind of legend about the desert Arabs with their inscrutable faces and meditative silences supposed to conceal depths of wisdom. They conceal nothing except stupidity. Sometimes a chief is encountered who has had a Western education, but he is alone in a vast horde of illiterates.

One of the hardest things to realize about these people is that none of them ever possessed a permanent home or resided in a house. They are born under a tent, they are brought up there, and they will die and be buried under a heap of stones. Their whole outlook on life has been the open plain, the sky, the storm, the rain, the fierce sun of the desert. The family, which means everything, has been centred round the group of tents.

These tents are not, as might be supposed, gorgeously decked residences. They consist of a kind of very large blanket made of coarse camel's and goat's hair. This blanket is stretched on posts and pegged down on three sides, leaving the fourth open. On the floor are placed rugs and carpets and a few hard cushions stuffed with millet.

When the nomad is married the tent is divided into two parts by another blanket and the man lives on one side and his wife and children on the other. When the camp is struck, the posts are removed, the blankets are rolled up and the whole is placed on the back of a camel or donkey.

This first expedition led Gertrude past Pisgah, where Balaam cursed Israel, and Moses' last resting place on Mount Nebo.

"The Moses legend is a very touching one," she wrote. "I stood on the top of Pisgah and looked out over the wonderful Jordan valley and the blue sea and the barren hills, veiled and beautified by cloud, and thought it was one of the most pathetic stories that I have ever been told."

And if Gertrude had been a reader of the Bible she would have seen how even more tragic was the fate of this great leader who, after endless patience with the Israelites, was forbidden to take them into the Promised Land because he once lost his temper with their eternal grumbling:

". . . and the Lord spake unto Moses," tells the Book of Deuteronomy, after Moses had been mercilessly sentenced: "Get thee up into this mountain unto Mount Nebo, which is in the land of Moab, which is over against Jericho; and behold the land of Canaan, which I give unto the children of Israel for a possession: And die in the mount and be gathered up unto thy people . . . And Moses went up from the plain of Moab unto the mountain of Nebo, to the top of Pisgah, which is over against Jericho. And the Lord shewed him all the land of Gilead unto Dan . . . And the Lord said unto him, This is the land which I sware unto Abraham, unto Isaac and unto Jacob, saying, I will give it unto thy seed: I have caused thee to see it with thine eyes, but thou shalt not go over thither. So Moses the servant of the Lord died there in the land of Moab, according to the word of the Lord. And He buried him in a valley in the land of Moab, over against Bethpeor: but no man knoweth of his sepulchre unto this day."

At Madeba she encountered an American press photographer who told her that if she was going any further inland she should have some sort of armed escort. Gertrude thanked the man and, rather against her will, called on the Turkish authorities and found them none too cordial and definitely suspicious. She later discovered that these suspicions were based on an idea that England had her eye on this part of the country, which, as things turned out, was not far wrong, though a little premature. Realizing that the situation called for tact she immediately became very feminine and helpless which, combined with the fact that she had a camera and was prepared to take pictures of the Turkish officials, smoothed all the difficulties away. This was Gertrude's first test of diplomatic ability to deal with Orientals and she bore it in mind for future occasions.

The next morning the escort appeared in the shape of a big, handsome, cheerful Circassian soldier mounted on a white stallion; and the little caravan set off. It must have been a pleasing picture, the daughter of the Yorkshire ironmaster, but lately at the Court of the Kaiser, riding her horse like a man with the good-looking escort at her side. Behind, the cook on a donkey and a motley collection of Bedouins churning up the dust as they followed the track which eventually leads to Mecca.

The vision of the gamekeeper on that July night thirty-two years before was beginning to materialize.

As a matter of fact it was just as well that Gertrude had taken the advice of the American photographer about the escort. Shortly after leaving the superb ruins of the seventh century palace of Chosroes I, which she had been photographing, three yelling tribesmen, armed to the teeth, came galloping towards the small procession. It looked like trouble. However, when the men saw the soldier they halted their charge, remained undecided for a moment and, with a curt greeting, rode away disgusted at losing what looked like a fine prize.

Gertrude's primary object in making this journey was to get the feel of travelling alone in the desert and to improve her Arabic, her second was to have some practical experience of archaeology which, up to date, she had only studied in theory. The palace of Chosroes was a feast of inscriptions and sent her enthusiastically to examine the Moabite town of King Sihon and the mighty crusader fort at Kerak. Following the old Roman roads she deciphered what was written on the milestones of the period and spent some hours beside the tomb of Aaron! She also found time to make careful notes about the desert tracks and the water points. Although the data seemed of little practical value to her at the time, some sort of instinct must have influenced her; for all the facts about the country which she compiled during these wanderings were found invaluable to the British

General Staff in 1915 and later to Lawrence when the war moved into Arabia and Palestine.

All this delving into dry archaeology and topography, studying the language, and harsh physical experiences did not erase any of the femininity or the romantic element in Gertrude. She wrote about the flowers of the desert and either wore them or kept them in a mug of water in her tent. None of the details about the Arab women, which would go unnoticed by a male explorer, escaped her and she saw and described the settings of the desert people with the mind of an artist.

"These people are gipsies," she wrote to her step-mother, "some of them have just been dancing for me round my camp fire. It was quite dark, with a tiny moon, the fire of dry thorns flickered up—faded and flickered again and showed the circle of men crouching on the ground, their black and white cloaks round them and the woman in the middle dancing. She looked as if she had stepped out of an Egyptian fresco. She wore a long red gown bound round her waist with a dark blue cloth, and falling open in front to show a redder petticoat below. Round her head was another blue cloth bound tightly and falling in long ends down her back, her chin was covered by a white cloth drawn up round her ears and falling in folds to her waist. Her feet, in red leather shoes, scarcely moved but all her body danced and she swept a red handkerchief she held in one hand, round her head, and clasped her hands together in front of her face. The men played a drum and a discordant fife and sang a monotonous song and clapped their hands and gradually she came nearer and nearer to me, twisting her slender body till she dropped on the heap of brushwood at my feet, and kneeling, her body still danced and her arms swayed and twisted round the mask-like face . . ."

At the beginning of April Gertrude began the return journey and reached Jericho on the 6th, describing the city as, in proportion to its size, having the largest proportion of mosquitoes and fleas of any inhabited spot of the globe!

The following week she was back in Jerusalem where she found a large quantity of mail from England to which she conscientiously replied, discussing Italian art with her sister who was in Florence as if she had no other interest than this subject!

CHAPTER VII

Gertrude rested in Jerusalem for three weeks and then set out again into the interior of Arabia. This time it was to be a journey of much more importance and hazard as she was to penetrate into the country of the Druze. One of the reasons which prompted her to go into a district, reputed to be dangerous to foreigners, was that the first person to visit the Djebel Druze had been an English-woman. In 1812 Lady Hester Stanhope, the niece of William Pitt, had penetrated into this country, then completely unknown to the outside world, and had become so attached to the people that she had settled among them and lived the last twenty years of her life on the slopes of Mount Lebanon.

The Druze are an interesting race. They are a mixture of Arab, Syrian, Kurdish and Turkoman blood and, although desert people, have always lived in mountainous districts. Belonging to an esoteric faith, founded in the eleventh century by Alhakim, the Fahtmid Caliph of Egypt, whose mother was a Russian, they believe in one God who has made himself known to men by successive incarnations. Jesus is accepted as one of these incarnations, but not Mohammed. An intelligent and hospitable people, the Druze are more crafty than the Arabs and harder to understand. Their rigid adherence to certain Islamic teachings cause them to keep their wives so strictly veiled that they do not even uncover their faces when in bed!

The Druze played an important part in the Great War by remaining neutral and causing a lot of uneasiness to the belligerents who did not know which side they would take until, eventually, in 1918, partly through Gertrude's influence and Lawrence's personality, they joined the allies and helped in the Revolt in the Desert.

Gertrude shared Lady Hester Stanhope's high opinion of the Druze and considered them to be a people worthier of trust than the Arabs. This was not the conviction of the Turkish authorities who were strongly opposed to any European, and certainly to a white woman, venturing into the Druze mountains. But the Turks did not know Gertrude or appreciate the hundred subtle ways she would approach a difficult problem. All they could see was a female who travelled like a male and treated the members of the opposite sex as equals. They did not suspect that she did this merely as a matter of convenience and when it came to a question of mind versus mind relied entirely on her woman's intuition.

Reaching a place called Bosrah, from which could be seen the volcanic peaks of the Djebel Druze, Gertrude called on the local governor and, to his questions as to her destination, replied that she was making for Damascus. This statement was received with an incredulous smile. Gertrude then added that she wished to go via Salkhad, which is in the heart of the Druze territory. The governor immediately objected that there was nothing to see in Salkhad. Gertrude said that she wanted to go there all the same. The governor again objected that the country was very dangerous. Gertrude did not mind. The governor paused, baffled by such obstinacy, and then said that he had received a message from Damascus forbidding him to authorize any foreigners, and particularly white women, to go into the Druze country. Gertrude knew that this was not true, but she pretended to be very disappointed and said that she quite understood and would remain in Bosrah. She returned to her camp and confided a plan to her cook.

The governor had evidently believed Gertrude as little as she had believed him, for towards evening a message came saying that he would pay her a call at sunset. Gertrude sent back a message that she had been taken ill and was retiring to bed. One hour later the governor appeared at the camp, but the cook told him that his lady was very sick and could see no one. The governor, not in the least convinced, inquired if the lady was marching on the morrow. The cook replied that he did not think so. The governor was nonplussed and after loitering about for a while said that Gertrude must on no account leave Bosrah without first seeing him. He then went back to his quarters.

At two o'clock in the morning Gertrude got up and, rousing her servants, quietly packed up the camp. It was bitterly cold as she paced up and down praying that no sentry would look over the castle walls. No sentry did and at three the little caravan was under way. There was no guide, but Gertrude had a rough map and hoped to pick up someone on the road. Time was lost getting clear of Bosrah's tortuous alleys and once she was stopped and thought that she would be held, but a little glib talk bluffed the gatekeepers and by dawn the party was away in the mountains and fairly safe from pursuit, as the soldiers would not venture into Druze country. Areh was reached at eight-thirty, where the Druze Sheik welcomed Gertrude and the welcome became an ovation when he heard of the hoodwinking of the governor of Bosrah. To everyone who came to call on this strange white woman the Sheik repeated the story of her getting the better of the hated Turkish authorities and this, combined with the legends of Lady Hester Stanhope, enhanced Gertrude's prestige and made of her visit a triumphal success.

She found the Druze to be intelligent, good-looking, charming people, whose hospitality was overwhelming; and during the ten days she spent among them she was feasted and entertained until she could hardly eat another mouthful.

A poet composed an ode in her honour and Gertrude, not quite knowing how to thank him, said that if someone in England wrote a poem about her she would give him a shilling. The Druze bard replied:

"Yes, it would happen."

So Gertrude gave him the equivalent of a shilling and he gave her the poem.

She was asked to the house of a very important sheik who had thought it a good idea to serve her tea in the English style. However, when it came to the actual making of the tea, he was extremely vague and inquired as to whether or not the milk should be boiled with the water!

A nargileh was offered her which she smoked, but she did not like it and was glad when it went out.

While accepting this hospitality she did not let herself forget that she had work to do. She collected all the information she could on desert tracks and water points, discovered some interesting ruins from which she copied the inscriptions and made a solemn pilgrimage to the grave of the prophet Job! When the time came for her to leave these reputedly savage tribesmen, they all flocked about her begging her to come back, and it was with regret that she travelled on to Damascus where she suddenly found herself in a cosmopolitan atmosphere, sleeping in a bed in an Occidental hotel.

Gertrude was not interested in Damascus and decided to make another expedition in a different direction, to Baalbec and the Cedars of Lebanon, then back to the coast at Beyrouth. This time the authorities made certain that she did not set out on her own and insisted on her taking an escort of Turkish soldiers with her. Part of the trip would be over desolate, waterless country, so, for the first time in Gertrude's travels, camels had to be included in the caravan.

The journey turned out to be much harder than expected, with long stages over a desert, burning hot in May, and few water points. The guide one day pointed out the caravan track which leads to Nejd, a forty-day trek without a spring or a well. One day Gertrude was to make for Nejd herself, but for the moment she was finding quite enough to cope with in the deserts of Syria. Sometimes her stages would take ten to twelve hours and on one occasion she was in the saddle for sixteen.

This ride was the first occasion when she realized that, although she was among people who should know their business in the desert, there were occasions when a little practical occidentalism did no harm.

Owing to the scarcity of water points, reserves of water had to be carried on the camels. On arrival one evening at a place called Kasr el Khair, after a comparatively leisurely ride but in great heat, it was found that two of the water skins had leaked and were quite empty, while one of the muleteers, in order to lighten the load of his animals, had emptied the contents of the skins which they carried onto the desert. The caravan thus found itself at a waterless camping site with ten animals and seven people, and nothing to drink beyond what was in their water bottles. The Arabs, with their fatalistic composure, were quite prepared to spend the night where they were, hope for the best, and in the morning, if God was willing, set out in search of a well. Gertrude considered the problem for a moment and, feeling that she had no convictions about the providence of God, decided to make for the nearest water point, reputed to be seven hours' march away. The Arabs stared at her incredulously when she suggested that the caravan should move on to the water, and took no further notice. She began to plead, then she threatened and finally mounted her horse and ordered the men to get on their way, and grumblingly the stage was covered before she would allow anyone to rest.

From that day on, the whole of Gertrude's attitude towards the members of her caravan altered. Up to that time she had felt that perhaps she was unseasoned in desert travel and the Arabs must know best. Now she understood that they were a people who had to be either led or driven, and when handled in this way all the nonsense about Destiny was forgotten.

But to know the psychological moment when patience must give way to action required an uncanny instinct. The Arabs will accept leadership or coercion only when every other roundabout method has been exhausted, and any exasperation during the process will lead to a blank wall of obstinacy. How accustomed Gertrude became to this mentality can be seen in letters when she describes, without comment, incidents which would have driven most Occidentals into raging hysterics:

"When I arrived I had asked if there were pack horses. 'As many as you like can be found,' said the innkeeper. Presently he returned to say that there were none. 'Then,' said I, 'I will take a cart to the village at the edge of the hills.' 'Most excellent,' said the surrounding company, 'the cart will draw you to the hills and then you will get camels.' 'Camels are to be found then?' said I. 'Many,' said they. Then arrived the Kaimakam and the Other, and I explained that I was leaving at once for Salur with my luggage in a cart. They heartily approved of this plan. Over the coffee the other let fall a remark to the effect that I should find no people at all as they had all gone up to Yaila. 'Then how shall I find camels?' said I. 'Effendim,' said he, 'there will be no camels.' Finally I resolved to *take* camels from him and after waiting for four hours the camels have appeared."

Immediately Gertrude reached the end of this gruelling stage she fell asleep and remained unconscious for eleven hours. To those who have not led a desert life this does not seem a particular feat for someone who is exhausted; but when one has tried to rest and undergone the torment of flies and other stinging insects, the heat, the noise of the other members of the caravan, who can sleep under any conditions and do not respect the privacy of their neighbours, it is not as easy as it sounds. Gertrude became impervious to noises and overcame the insect pest by having made for herself a huge muslin bag into which she crept when she wanted to rest. She never let this contrivance out of her sight, though she said that if her camp was attacked by a "ghazu" of Arabs, her flight would be as one who runs a sack race!

While still maintaining her authority over her followers when it was necessary, she conformed in every possible way to the traditions and the customs of the Arabs. This was not always too easy and there were occasions when she inadvertently made breaches of etiquette. On this particular journey she nearly estranged the sympathy of a very important sheik.

Arriving at a big water point, she found a whole tribe of Bedouins watering their flocks. The sheik at once made himself known and invited her to take coffee with him, and she joined the circle before the black tent. She sat for some time listening to the desert gossip, until she began to feel helplessly sleepy. No one was paying the slightest attention to her, so she got up quietly and slipped away to her camp. Hardly had she reached it when one of her own men hurried up and informed her that she had committed a fearful solecism. Apparently the sheik had killed a sheep in her honour and expected her to dine. Gertrude was filled with consternation and asked her retainer what she should do. The man replied that she must give a present and return to the circle. Now, the only gifts which any Arab of importance will consider are arms or horses. Gertrude was not going to give away a horse so she went into her tent and, wrapping her pistol in a silk handkerchief, sent it over to the sheik. Peace was made and Gertrude sleepily returned to the circle and waited two hours for dinner to be served.

This meal procedure of desert Arabs, to those not acquainted with the ways of Bedouins, is at first difficult to understand. To begin with the nomad has only one meal a day. When he rises in the morning, he will drink a cup of coffee or mint tea; and, if hungry in the middle of the day, a handful of dates will suffice him. It is not until the sun is setting and he can relax that he settles down to serious eating. The meal usually consists of a highly spiced soup served in a common bowl, into which everyone dips with a wooden spoon, followed by a dish of meat and vegetables, which is eaten from the dish with the fingers, and the dinner invariably ends with a huge platter of what an Occidental would call semolina. Water or the milk of sheep or goats is drunk, with coffee and tea later in the evening. That is the ordinary dinner for a Bedouin, but when an important stranger comes to the camp a much more elaborate repast is prepared. If the coming of the guest is known beforehand, the dinner is ready when he arrives, but if, as in Gertrude's case, he appears unexpectedly the same feast will be served which takes a considerable time. A visiting sheik is aware of this procedure and like all Arabs, having no sense of time, is quite prepared to wait until it is time to eat. At this period of her desert journeying Gertrude was not fully versed in Bedouin lore and probably did not appreciate that she was regarded as an honoured guest, and her ignorance cost her a pistol.

The cooking of this special dinner takes literally many hours; for, in addition to all kinds of meat stews and sausage rolls and sickly almond paste cakes, there is invariably a sheep roast whole. The sheep is alive and peacefully browsing when the honoured, but unexpected, guest descends on the camp, so that it has to be captured, killed, skinned, cleaned and roasted on a spit over the embers of a brushwood fire before the guests can assemble before the tent to dine. The long wait is, however, well worth while, as Gertrude discovered, for there is no meat more delicious than that of the sheep laid before the guests in its entirety. No knives or forks are used and the diners expertly pick tasty morsels from the carcass with their fingers.

Apart from this small social error, the expedition was lacking in incident. Gertrude continued her journey, mapping and making records of ruins, until she eventually reached Lebanon. For a few days she camped at Aflea, where the river Adonis, legendary place of the meeting of Venus and her lover, springs out of a great cave. From the forests of Lebanon she collected a number of cedar cones and took them to England, and today, in the grounds of Rounton Grange, a real cedar of Lebanon, descendant of the trees about which King Solomon wrote, rears its evergreen head to the Yorkshire skies.

Then all of a sudden an urge came over Gertrude to go home and see her parents and she travelled by forced marches to Beyrouth and on to Jaffa where she could find a ship. There was no idea of deserting Arabia, just a passing nostalgia for her own kind, and she wrote to her father before sailing:

> ". . . we shall go to Jaffa tomorrow, as there is a boat and I am anxious to get home. But you know, dearest father, I shall be back before long. One doesn't keep away from the East when one has been in so far . . ."

Gertrude had only been in Arabia for just over six months, but she had absorbed more than the average traveller in six years. She had allowed the desert and its people to take possession of her heart, and she knew that it was only a matter of time before she settled for ever among the vague, friendly wanderers of these stony wildernesses.

CHAPTER VIII

When Gertrude abandoned the white glare of the desert for the gentler green of England in early summer, she found an unbelievable change.

The Victorian era was a thing of the past, the Boer War was dragging itself to a weary conclusion and Great Britain, disillusioned by the attitude of Continental Europeans during her struggle in South Africa, was realizing that imperial isolation might sound all right, but it was no longer practical.

The dying of the nineteenth century had passed unnoticed by Gertrude in the midst of Arabs and Druze, but a complete metamorphosis, at first not generally appreciated, had come over the world.

Sensing this quickly she adapted herself more easily to the new tempo than those who had remained at home. While the reign of Edward VII was not to bring her into public prominence, it was to establish her among a group of men who realized the importance of her investigations in the Near East. Some of these were archaeologists, some were politicians . . . a number belonged to the military profession.

However, for the moment, there was no question of serious international disturbances and Gertrude settled down to a quiet life in England. In fact, she did an unprecedented thing in remaining in the country for a whole year, giving herself up to County life.

But that was as long as her wandering instinct could remain dormant, and in July of 1902 she went to Switzerland to climb the Finsteraarhorn, a peak respected by the most hardened Alpinists. She made her headquarters at Meiringen where she conferred with her guides as to the best plan for attacking the mountain and, having settled the details, waited for a suitable day.

At one-thirty in the morning, early in August, the start was made. The first part of the ascent was across dangerous slopes, down which unheralded avalanches of stones made progress risky. Then into rock chimneys and granitc towers which required strength as well as skill to scale. So far there were no mishaps, but at two in the afternoon the weather began to look threatening. The guides paused in their scrambling and anxiously scanned the black clouds which were rolling up, but Gertrude was not ready to give in and the climb continued. By three the trio was within a thousand feet of the summit and in spite of snow flurries a final effort was made to reach the peak. But the weather rapidly grew worse and, finding themselves faced with pinnacles of rock coated with ice, the guides insisted that it would be suicidal to go on. Gertrude had to reluctantly agree and the retreat began.

Even now the decision seemed to have been taken too late as the clouds completely shrouded the mountain and the snow storm developed into a blizzard which, with the oncoming night, made it impossible to see more than a few feet ahead. There seemed little chance of the party getting back safely.

Gertrude's own words vividly tell of the perils through which she and her guides passed during that descent.

"We toiled on till eight, by which time a furious thunderstorm was raging. We were standing by a great upright on the top of a tower when suddenly it gave a crack and a blue flame sat on it for a second. My ice axe jumped in my hand and I thought the steel felt hot through my woollen glove. Before we knew where we were the rock flashed again, it was a great sticking out stone and I expect it attracted the lightning, but we didn't stop to consider this theory but stumbled down a chimney as hard as ever we could, one on top of the other, buried our ice axes in some shale at the bottom of it and hurriedly retreated from them. It's not nice to carry a private lightning conductor in your hand in the thick of a thunderstorm.

"It was quite clear we could go no further that night, the question was to find the best lodging while there was still light to see. We hit upon a tiny crack sheltered from the wind, even the snow did not fall into it. There was just room for me to sit in the extreme back of it on a very pointed bit of rock; by doubling up I could even get my head into it. Ulrich sat on my feet to keep them warm and Heinrich just below. At first the thunderstorm made things rather exciting. The claps followed the flashes so close that there seemed no interval between them. We tied ourselves firmly onto the rock above lest, as Ulrich philosophically said, one of us should be struck and fall out. The rocks were all crackling round us and fizzing like damp wood which is just beginning to burn. It's a curious exciting sound rather exhilarating, and as there was no further precaution possible I enjoyed the extraordinary magnificence of the storm with a free mind: it was worth seeing. Gradually the night cleared and became beautifully starry. Between two and three the moon rose, a tiny crescent, and we spoke of the joy it would be when the sun rose full on us and stopped our shivering. But the sun never rose at all, at least for all practical purposes. The day came wrapped in a blinding mist and heralded by a cutting, snow-laden wind; we never saw the sun in it. I can scarcely describe to you what the day was like. We were from four A.M. to eight P.M. on the *arête*; during that time we ate for a minute or two three times and my fare I know was five gingerbread biscuits, two sticks of chocolate, a slice of bread, a scrap of cheese and a handful of raisins. We had nothing to drink but two tablespoonfuls of brandy in the bottom of my flask and a mouthful of wine in the guides' wine skin, but it was too cold to feel thirsty. There was scarcely a yard which we could come down without the extra rope. But both ropes were thoroughly iced and terribly difficult to manage, the weather was appalling. It was rather interesting to see the way the mountain behaved in a snowstorm and how avalanches are born and all the wonderful and terrible things that happen in high places . . ."

And so the descent of the mountain went on, foot by foot. Gertrude and her guides had hoped to make some sort of shelter that evening, but their progress was so slow that they had to spend another night crouching on a ledge of rock. Even then she did not complain:

"I consoled myself by thinking of Maurice in South Africa," she remarked, "and how he had slept out in the pouring rain and been none the worse . . ."

But if Gertrude made light of her adventure on these sleet-swept slopes, hardened climbers of the Alpine Club appreciated the feat which she had accomplished. Captain Farrar, writing in the *Alpine Journal*, said:

"The vertical height of the rock face measured from the glacier to the summit of the mountain is about 3,000 feet. There can be in the whole Alps few places so steep and so high. The climb has only been done three times, including Miss Bell's attempt, and it is still considered one of the greatest expeditions in the whole Alps. Her strength, incredible in that slim frame, her endurance, above all her courage, were so great that even to this day her guide and companion Ulrich Fuhrer speaks with admiration of her that amounts to veneration. He told the writer, some years ago, that of all the amateurs, men or women, that he had travelled with, he had seen but very few to surpass her in technical skill and none to equal her in coolness, bravery and judgement."

Speaking of this descent of the Finsteraarhorn, Ulrich Fuhrer used to say:

"When the freezing wind beats you almost to the ground, when the blizzard nearly blinds you, half paralyzing your senses, when the cold is so intense that the snow freezes on you as it falls, clothing you in a sheet of ice, till life becomes insupportable—then, indeed, was Miss Bell pre-eminent."

He might have added, that when the sandstorm smothered everything, blotting out the landscape in its fiery path, when death from thirst or from sunstroke would have been a blessed relief from the torment of the desert, Miss Bell showed more fortitude than Arabs born to the merciless climate of Arabia. Gertrude's physique was not masculine and if she endured hardships which would have broken the resistance of many men, it was because of that tenacious spirit which did not know the meaning of defeat. It was a peculiar characteristic, as most men and women given to occupations which require bodily resistance have correspondingly weak minds. But Gertrude's brain was in every way equal to her physical endurance.

In the autumn the East called again and she visited Smyrna, Magnesia, Burnabat and Haifa, settling for a while at Mount Carmel. She took up Persian once more, but did not venture into the wilds, and concentrated on dialects and tribal customs.

Returning to England for a brief spell, she started round the world for a second time at the end of the year; making her first stop at Delhi for King Edward's Durbar. She was accompanied this time by her step-brother Hugo. He was considerably younger, having gone to Eton when Gertrude was in Persia. Although devoted to each other, the brother and sister had diverging conceptions of life. Gertrude's brilliant and energetic mind wanted proof of anything which was not clear before she would accept a solution. Religion meant nothing to her, being unable to reconcile obvious facts with the theories dogmatically laid down by the Church. Hugo was inclined to be an idealist and a conscientious believer in Christianity as a solution to all problems. Gertrude used to argue with her brother about these beliefs, but with that tenacious Bell character he remained unmoved and, not long after the return from the world cruise, he was ordained a clergyman of the Church of England.

Although Gertrude was to be in India for quite a short time, she started to learn Hindustani and tried to form some idea of the problems which confronted the natives and their British rulers. She was impressed by the magnificence of the Durbar and the spectacle of India paying homage to its King Emperor. She was shocked by the aloof attitude of the British to the Indians and amused at the way in which suburban English life was transplanted to a land where it was quite unsuited. She stayed in native states with Maharajahs, and rode elephants which she did not like as much as camels. She mixed with wild tribesmen of the Frontier at Peshawar, and from Darjeeling saw the sun rise over Everest. Then on to Burmah and up the Irrawaddy in a small boat. She made friends with Buddhist monks and Burmese dancing girls. Thence she moved south to the Dutch Indies, to the Malay States and to Hongkong. China delighted her and she spent some time in Shanghai trying to get to know the Chinese whom she misjudged completely. The Boxer Rebellion and massacres were but lately over and she recorded that the country had settled down to an era of peace and goodwill to the foreigners!

From China a ship took her to Port Arthur where she enjoyed the Russians and saw the twilight of the Czarist imperial régime in the Far East. In less than two years the Japanese would have driven the Russians out of Manchuria and an ex-Worcester naval cadet, called Togo, would be forming a navy to menace the rest of the world. But neither Gertrude nor Hugo foresaw this, in fact Hugo became convinced that Russia was on the eve of taking over the control of Asia. Japan was also seen just before it became a Power which counted, but Gertrude did not seem to appreciate why the Japanese were so cordial to all Britons! Their character she misconstrued, dismissing them as charming little people who had lovely gardens and smiled all the time.

Although Gertrude's letters from the Far East are not very detailed, they are filled with astute comment, but it is the comment of a spectator and not, as in her correspondence from Arabia, that of one of the people. It is not clear as to whether she neglected her study of Chinese and Japanese history or was merely not interested in their politics, but she does not seem to have realized that she was in those countries on the eve of a crisis which would alter the history of the world.

She sailed from Yokohama to Vancouver and travelled east via the Canadian Rockies. Her first natural impulse, on finding herself in the midst of these giants among mountains, was to climb a peak, and to her joyous surprise she discovered three Swiss guides with whom she had made ascents in the Oberland. Her pleasure was only equalled by that of the guides and, to climax the trip round the world, she conquered one of the highest peaks of the Rocky Mountains.

The rest of 1903 and 1904 was spent in Europe, chiefly in Yorkshire and London, with visits to Paris and Berlin. For the moment all idea of travelling and exploration was forgotten; everyone was eager to meet her and there were few nights when she did not dine at some fashionable house in Paris or London.

At one dinner party she sat next the Agha Khan, the direct descendant of Mohammed, but a "bon viveur" and one of the richest men in the world. When Gertrude told him that she was thinking of going to Baghdad he remarked:

"Let me know if you go as I would like to give you letters to my uncles who guard the Shrine at Kerbela. The Marlborough Club always finds me."

The holy places at Kerbela, the Marlborough Club, Mohammed, a smart dinner in London . . . such a mixture could only be possible in the British Empire.

She met Sargent, who later was to do her portrait, and discussed Greek art with him.

Salomon Reinach, the eminent archaeologist and Orientalist, asked her over to Paris to give her opinion on some valuable Byzantine MSS. which he had acquired. They wandered together through the Oriental rooms of the Louvre and studied Greek "first editions" in the Bibliothèque Nationale. A week later she was climbing the Matterhorn from the Italian side, one of the most difficult ascents of the Alps.

Gertrude was now thirty-four. She had seen practically the whole of the world, and while Arabia interested her and absorbed her thoughts she seemed to hesitate before finally deciding to devote the rest of her life to the study of that country. The memory of Henry Cadogan was still alive and the recollections of those happy days in Tehran kept her mind on that part of Asia. In a letter addressed to her cousin Edward Stanley, who was civil commissioner to Nigeria, she revealed what was passing through her mind:

> ". . . Marcus Aurelius is a good counsellor, if one can follow his advice. I mostly find myself rebelling against it, with an uncanny sense of being too hopelessly involved in the mortal coil to profit by it. What is the use of bending all one's energies to the uncongenial thing? One is likely to do little enough anyway, but if one's time is taken up persuading oneself one likes it or at least conquering a distaste there is very little left to achieve success with. Find the thing that needs no such preparatory struggle and then do it for all you are worth, if you can. There will always be black or gray moments when it is sufficiently difficult to do even the thing you like . . ."

Gertrude did not take long to make up her mind what she wanted to do "for all she was worth"; she had undoubtedly decided long ago, and in January of 1905 she set out for Syria. As if trying to test her metal, her initial welcome back to the Near East was a sharp bout of fever, but still inexperienced in this side of Oriental life she dismissed the attack as she might a cold. The fever temporarily accepted the rebuff and left the arrogant Englishwoman to her

Arab friends who received her with the enthusiasm of children.

Her objective this time was another Druze district and she had the usual difficulty with the government authorities who seemed determined to hamper her expeditions. However, now thoroughly understanding cumbrous Turkish officialdom, she got away without trouble and abandoned herself to the triumphant welcome of the desert.

Without any waste of time she assembled her caravan and came quickly to the borders of the Druze country. She just missed a terrific ghazu raid, for, coming to the camp of the Beni Hassan tribe, she found that five hundred horsemen had carried off two thousand sheep and all the tents the day before. Gertrude sympathized with those who had been plundered and asked them what they were going to do about it. The survivors of the raid replied resignedly that they would first of all make the rounds of the neighbouring tribes and borrow a camel here and a camel there and a few tents. When they were rehabilitated, they would bide their time until they were organized and then collect a band of horsemen and raid the raiders. By this means they would probably regain all they had lost! Gertrude, commenting on this, remarked:

> "It seems a most unreasonable industry, this of ghazu—about as profitable as stealing each other's washing, but that is how they live."

The tribe, however, did not seem to take the raid much to heart, for the next day was the Mohammedan Feast of Sacrifice when three camels would be eaten. The camp was festooned with white shirts as this was the yearly occasion of great washing. As soon as the sun set, the Arabs began firing their rifles into the air with deafening reports and Gertrude, feeling that she must take some part in the ritual, stood at the door of her tent periodically letting off her revolver!

A few days later she saw the preparation for the reprisal raid.

Dining in her tent at the foot of a great ruined castle set in the crater of an extinct volcano, she was suddenly disturbed by shouting and the firing of guns. She came out of her tent and saw fires burning on the turrets of the castle signalling to the tribes in the desert to assemble. The walls were already crowded with warriors who brandished clubs and swords which glistened in the moonlight, and chanted a warlike song:

"O Lord our God! Upon them! Upon them! Let the child leave his mother's side, let the young man mount and be gone!"

Gertrude scrambled up the rocky slope to join in the ceremony, and as the sheiks saw her they cried out:

"Upon thee be peace! The English and the Druze are one!"

To which Gertrude replied, not knowing why, but feeling that something must be said:

"Praise be to God! We too are a fighting race."

The Druze cheered and abandoned themselves once more to their Pagan ritual, which must have made Mohammed shiver in his grave and wonder whether his years of hardship, trying to teach his followers to love one another, had been worth while. Long into the night, after Gertrude had gone to bed, the wild chanting continued, until, exhausted, the warriors fell asleep where they stood, and rested for a while before setting out on their murderous mission to recapture their flocks and kill every man, woman and child of the Sakhr tribe whom they might come across.

And in contrast to this barbaric ceremony, Gertrude found herself a few days later drinking coffee with another sheik and discussing the victories of the Japanese over the Russians and the possible repercussions which the defeat of an Occidental power by Orientals might bring about. A problem which would touch Gertrude very closely ten years later when the armies of Great Britain were not doing so well against the Turks and it was not easy to convince the Arabs of England's might. For the moment there was no question of this and the conversation drifted on from Togo's naval successes to the death of Lord Salisbury and an analysis of Joseph Chamberlain, while Gertrude explained the fiscal question so clearly in Arabic that her Druze listeners became Free Traders on the spot!

Gertrude was in no way a propagandist for Great Britain, but she realized that the Druzes were not too contented and recorded in her *Desert and the Sown:*

> "Nevertheless, the moral is obvious: all over Syria and even in the desert, whenever a man is ground down by injustice or mastered by his own incompetence, he wishes he were under the rule that has given wealth to Egypt, and our occupation of that country, which did so much at first to alienate from us the sympathies of Mohammedans, has proved the finest advertisement of English methods of government."

She did not spend much time in the Druze country as it was freezingly cold, and after checking her maps, marking water points and copying a few inscriptions she returned to

Damascus. She found the government authorities relieved to see her safely back and also most interested to hear about Druze affairs. But Gertrude was cautious in her replies, feeling that any indiscretion might lose her the intimacy which she was building up with the desert tribes. At the same time she was gratified to find that she was now being treated seriously and no longer regarded as a crazy female.

As soon as the weather grew a little warmer she set off again, this time into Asia Minor. She revisited Baalbek, passed through Kuseir and Homa until she came to Kalaat el Husn. She had ridden for ten and a half hours with an escort of two mounted Kurds and a couple of handcuffed deserters who were being taken to prison.

One of the prisoners was very talkative.

" 'Lady, lady,' he asked, 'have you journeyed to the land of Hind?'

" 'Yes,' said I.

" 'May God make it Yes upon you! Have you heard there of a great king Mohammed?'

"Again I was able to reply in the affirmative and even to add that I myself knew him, for their King Mohammed was no other than my fellow subject the Agha Khan, and the religion of the prisoners boasted a respectable antiquity, having been founded by him whom we call the Old Man of the Mountain.

"Khudr caught my stirrup with his free hand and said eagerly:

" 'Is he not a great king?'

"But I answered cautiously, for though the Agha Khan is something of a great king in a modern sense, that is to say he is exceedingly wealthy, it would have been difficult to explain to his disciples exactly what the polished, well bred man of the world was like whom I had last met at a London dinner party and had given me the Marlborough Club as his address. Not that these things, if they could have understood them, would have shocked them; the Agha Khan is law unto himself, and if he chose to indulge in far greater excesses than dinner parties his actions would be sanctified by the mere fact that they were his.

"His father used to give letters of introduction to the Angel Gabriel in order to secure for his clients a good place in Paradise; the son with his English education and his familiarity with European thought, has refrained from exercising this privilege, though he has not ceased to hold, in the opinion of his followers, the keys of heaven. They show their belief in him in a substantial manner by subscribing, in various parts of Asia and Africa, a handsome income that runs yearly into tens of thousands."

Five hours before reaching Kalaat el Husn she could see in the distance the magnificent Crusader castle which is almost as big as Windsor. As the little caravan drew near, the whole edifice seemed to dominate the surrounding country and Gertrude halted for a moment to stare up at the massive walls which had defied centuries, before approaching the huge gateway which guarded a broad winding stair up which she rode with her escort. For an appreciable time the horses stumbled along over the dilapidated steps in almost complete darkness until, after passing six more great gateways, they came to a vast courtyard in the centre of the keep. Here Gertrude was received by the local chief who was most cordial and would not let her pitch her camp and provided instead spacious, if rather bare, accommodations. After introductions to various notables, all of whom lived in the castle, she was presented to two other women guests. One of these was an old Moslem woman and the other a Christian, wife of a government official. The son of the Mohammedan lady had but lately been murdered in a desert feud, but she did not seem to take it to heart, for when Gertrude asked her about it she merely replied:

"Murder is like the drinking of milk here, like the drinking of water."

And so the journey went leisurely on, through Kalaat Simian and Konia and Payas and Adana. Gertrude was more or less following the beaten track and, having temporarily given up surveying in favour of archaeology, was in no hurry. Her mind was set on ruins and finding inscriptions, which she carefully copied, whether she understood them or not. Her life motif was tending towards the academic but without making her lose touch with the people among whom she travelled. Writing to Florence Lascelles, she says:

> "What a country this is! I fear I shall spend the rest of my life travelling in it. Race after race, one on top of the other, the whole land strewn with the mighty relics of them. We in Europe are accustomed to think that civilisation is an advancing flood that has gone steadily forward since the beginning of time. I believe we are wrong. It is a tide that ebbs and flows, reaches a high water mark and turns back again. Do you think that from age to age it rises higher than before? I wonder—and I doubt."

She still lived in her camp, frequented the company of the natives and underwent great hardships to seek out Roman or Syrian remains of particular interest. She was also perfecting her Turkish which was to become useful during the war.

At this point an Arab came into her life who was to remain with her for nearly twenty years. His name was Fattuh and he had been cook to an Englishman called Lloyd who handed him over to Gertrude as the kind of trustworthy factotum whom she might need during her expeditions into the desert.

Oriental servants either are rascals with no loyalty and no scruples about betraying their employers, or are so devoted they will literally sacrifice themselves in the interests of their masters. Fattuh belonged to the latter variety and it is to be wondered how Gertrude could have carried on had it not been for this Arab to whom nothing counted before his mistress's well-being. Within a week of taking him into her service, Gertrude wrote:

> "And Fattuh, bless him! the best servant I have ever had, ready to cook my dinner or push a mule or dig out an inscription with equal alacrity and to tell me endless tales of travel as we ride, for he began life as a muleteer at the age of ten and knows every inch of ground from Aleppo to Van and Baghdad."

By the middle of May 1905 she had done all the excavating she wanted and returned to Konia, prior to embarking for England. Here she met, for the first time, Sir William Ramsay, one of the greatest authorities on the ruins and inscriptions of Asia Minor. To begin with, his attitude towards Gertrude was condescending, but after talking to her for a while he was so impressed by her knowledge and the instinct with which she had collected her inscriptions that he begged her to become his collaborator. This she could not do at once, but two years later she joined him and was actually able to put him on the way to finding an inscription for which he had been searching for years.

A few days after this meeting she embarked for Europe.

CHAPTER IX

Gertrude reached England in June of 1905 and immediately went to Yorkshire. She spent most of the summer in the country perfecting her famous rock garden and entertaining house parties.

Among the special friends who stayed at Rounton Grange was Captain Frederick O'Connor [1] who had just come back from the taking of Lhassa where he had acted as interpreter to Sir Francis Younghusband. After the signing of the treaty with the Thibetans he had remained as British representative among this mysterious people, and knew more about them than any other Occidental. He was about the same age as Gertrude and had the same thorough knowledge of the Indian Frontier as she of Arabia.

This interest in eastern countries, at that time practically unknown, created a bond in common and there were rumours of an engagement. But Gertrude did not marry Frederick O'Connor, or any of the other men who would have liked to marry her, chiefly because of her own attitude to the question. In the first place there was always that mental reserve about the man to whom she had once given her whole heart. But that was by no means a real obstacle and only made it impossible for her to love completely.

[1] Later, Lieutenant Colonel Sir Frederick O'Connor, C.S.I., C.I.E., C.V.O.

The real difficulty was her own arbitrary personality; she would not and could not genuinely subordinate herself to anyone. A man who married her would have to think and act according to her lights, and although this state of mind is now not uncommon in the Occident, regardless of whether the individual woman is superior to her mate or not, it was not understood in England of the early nineteen hundreds. Gertrude had to rule and guide and decide. There was no bluff about this determination, for whether it was a matter of a forced march in the desert or the appointment of an administrator to a new country—and she was convinced that she was right—no obstacle could deflect her from her course. Already the autocratic look and the firm mouth which characterize Sargent's picture of her, made some years later, were beginning to take the place of the young girl's laughing eyes and eager lips. Since those rose-scented nights in Tehran, no man had ruffled her peace of mind, and unless someone would be her partner, with the distinct understanding that she was the mistress, in every sense of the word, it seemed silly to marry.

For the moment thoughts of marriage or spinsterhood did not worry her. She was with her family, and old friends, enjoying the English summer. In the autumn she went again to Paris to visit Salomon Reinach and tell him of all she had discovered during the course of her last trip to Asia Minor, and obtain data for her next expedition. The whole of 1906 she gave to the writing of her first travel book, *The Desert and the Sown,* which Heinemann published the following year.

Then off again with her father to Egypt where Hugo joined them. In Cairo she met Lord Cromer who was, in regard to Egypt, what Gertrude was to be to Arabia and Mesopotamia. Lord Cromer was on the eve of his retirement, after twenty-four years as an administrator of Egypt, and was amazed to find what a great deal Gertrude knew about the Near East. She too wanted to learn all she could about Egypt and was put into touch with the head of the Azhar, the famous Mohammedan university of Cairo. She went to call on the learned man, and had hardly entered the building when she encountered an old friend of her wanderings in the Arabian peninsula who introduced her to the dignitaries of the university who, in turn, treated her as one of them—as usual a strange mixture of social and erudite occupations.

"Yesterday we lunched with the Bernstorffs," she writes home, "and we are going to their box at the opera tonight. On Friday, Father and I spent the whole morning with Ernest Richmond, seeing Coptic churches—most pleasant."

Sir Hugh Bell returned to England and in April of 1907 Gertrude was back in Asia Minor. This time her objectives were the cities of Ancient Greece: Magnesia, Miletus, Isbarta . . . where she wished to obtain some inscriptions for Professor Ramsay. The weather was wet, the rivers swollen by rain and many of the bridges swept away. But the mere crossing of a torrent with the water well over her boots did not bother Gertrude.

Asia Minor left a strong impression on her:

"Monotonous, colourless, lifeless," she wrote, "unsubdued by a people whose thoughts travel no further than the next furrow, who live and die and leave no mark upon the great plains and the barren hills—such is central Asia, of which this country is a true part. And that is why the Roman roads make such a deep impression on one's mind. They impressed the country itself, they implied a great domination, they tell of a people that overcame the general stagnation . . .

"It was very still and hot; clouds of butterflies drifted across the path and there was no other living thing except a stork or two in the marshy ground and here and there a herd of buffaloes with a shepherd boy asleep beside them. At the end of the lake a heavy thunderstorm gathered and crept along the low hills to the east and up into the middle of the sky. And so we came to the earliest record of what was probably one of the earliest trade roads in the world and the forerunner of the Roman road; and here the clouds broke upon us in thunder and lightning and hail and rain and I saw the four Hittite kings, carved in the massive stone, against a background of all the fury of the storm. They are seated by the edge of a wide pool, a spring bubbling out of the hillside, from which a swift river flows away to the lake; and above them are figures with uplifted hands, as though they praised the God of Gotat waters . . ."

At the end of May, Professor and Lady Ramsay unexpectedly joined Gertrude. They were accompanied by their son Louis, who had been commissioned by the British Museum to collect natural history specimens from these parts. Gertrude was busy excavating a church when the Ramsays suddenly appeared in two carts. The professor at once joined Gertrude while Lady Ramsay, the practical English-woman unaffected by her wild surroundings, set about preparing tea.

The church in which Gertrude was digging was comparatively modern and she had not yet learned that in Asia Minor there is never a shrine but, if one looks long enough, a holy place dating from the beginning of history will be found. Near this particular ruin Gertrude had discovered an inscription which she could not read and which was evidently not Christian. She had, however, copied down what appeared to be hieroglyphics and rather diffidently showed them to the professor. Sir William glanced at the notebook, stared, became alert and nearly leaped into the air. What Gertrude had showed him was a Hittite inscription which he had felt sure was in these parts, but had never been able to find. Gertrude glowed with pride as she sat over the teapot with Lady Ramsay, who was much more concerned over the impossibility of making good tea with desert water than over the writings of the Hittites.

Sir William and Gertrude now worked as close collaborators and the professor soon found that he had to have his wits alert to keep pace with his pupil. The party moved on to Daile and Karadagh and Karpuna, making archaeological history until, at the end of June, Lady Ramsay insisted on taking her family home. Gertrude, who was enthralled with her digging, remained until the heat drove her out and then made her way to Constantinople where she stayed at the British Embassy and was given an audience by the Grand Vizier.

As soon as she got back to London she was asked to submit her surveys to the Royal Geographical Society, and the Fellows were astonished to find that the material which she had collected, without any training or technical knowledge, was of immense scientific value. As a result of this she was given a course in astronomy, the use of the compass and the general principles of topography. This training enabled her to make more elaborate maps during her next journeys and the Geographical Society used her reports to complete their records on the Arabian Peninsula. From this date on she was able to lay just claim to the title of explorer, which is technically admissible only when the traveller, penetrating into unmapped territory, uses scientific instruments.

She did not return to the East at once and spent most of the year of 1908 writing in collaboration with Sir William Ramsay a remarkable book about the ruins of Asia Minor called *The Thousand and One Churches.*

The following year she travelled to Aleppo and thence down the Euphrates to Hit and across the desert to the Tigris. Her objective was the castle of Ukhaidir. Little was known about Ukhaidir, but from the ruins Gertrude was able to reconstruct the immense castle and wrote a detailed book about what she found with elaborate plans and maps. The book was not published until 1914, when her mind was turned to the more serious matter of the war, but among archaeologists it added to her already established reputation as an authority on the ruins of Asia Minor.

Once more going back to England at the end of that year, Gertrude became interested in something in no way connected with travel or archaeology.

Mrs. Pankhurst had set out militantly to place female suffrage on the statutes of England. The government was opposed to any parliamentary reform of this nature and the majority of the public either ridiculed the idea or was apathetic. But Mrs. Pankhurst was a determined woman and, with her followers, staged demonstrations, invaded the homes of cabinet ministers and became a menace to local peace.

Gertrude's step-mother, with Mrs. Humphry Ward and Lady Jersey, was strongly opposed to the suffragette campaign and, with the support of Lord Curzon and Lord Cromer, formed the Woman's Anti-Suffrage League. It might have been supposed that, after the years which Gertrude had spent among people who treated their women more or less like beasts of burden, she would have sided with the suffragettes; on the contrary, she gave her full allegiance to the step-mother's group for the fight against the rights of women.

It was another example of how essentially feminine she was at heart. From her point of view males were males and females females, with their respective rôles in life. Even in later years when it fell to her lot to have to govern men, she did so with the subtleties of a woman.

However, her interest in the anti-suffrage movement was quite temporary. The charm of the desert was weaving itself more and more about her heart and her absences from its wandering people were becoming shorter and shorter.

Nineteen hundred and eleven marks the beginning of Gertrude's claim to a place among great explorers. The preliminary ventures had attracted attention because they had been undertaken by a woman alone, but they had given nothing of any value to scientists or geographers. Gertrude, realizing this, now made up her mind to attack Arabia and carry her conquests farther than Palgrave or Doughty.

On her way East she paused in Rome to "complete her archaeological studies" but found that she was now regarded as a "professor" herself. Robert Hichens, then at the height of his fame, came to hear her lecture, and her audiences were composed of some of the greatest authorities in Italy, who wanted to learn from her.

By the beginning of the year she was in Damascus making ready for the hazardous crossing of the Syrian Desert.

This expedition had to be carefully prepared as she would be dependent for everything on her own caravan, and the mules and horses and camels had to be selected with the utmost care. By a piece of good fortune she fell in with an Arab postman and guide called Ali who had an invaluable experience of desert travelling and personal connections with many of the nomad chiefs. The combination of this man and Fattuh gave Gertrude a greater feeling of security than a battalion of soldiers and enabled her to leave the organization and protection of her caravan to them and concentrate on her surveying.

It was early February and bitterly cold when everything was ready. Being a Yorkshire girl, brought up in the rigorous climate of the north of England, Gertrude thought that she would be impervious to cold, but she did not yet know one aspect of the desert.

There is no freezing temperature which can convey such pain and grief as that of the rolling expanses of Arabia. The majority of people regard the desert as a waste of stones and sand where there is no means of keeping cool. This majority is, generally speaking, right, but when it is cold it is worse than the most torrid periods. The wind whistles through the scrub, cutting into the thickest garments and, with a complete absence of trees, there is no means of sheltering. The camels and the horses and the Arabs become mentally and physically numb and there seems to be no way to revive the blood circulation. The traveller wishes he were dead, and as one of Gertrude's sheik companions said with chattering teeth:

"By the head of your father! How can you leave the garden of the world and come out into this wilderness?"

There were times during this crossing of the Syrian Desert when the little water which the caravan carried froze, and the water skins had to be thawed over fires before filling; when snow and sleet fell and the muleteers lost courage and refused to leave their tents and continue the march. Gertrude, frozen to the bone, would argue and threaten, until finally, realizing that words were useless, she would pull out the pegs of the tent and bring it billowing down on the occupants who had to get out.

There were occasions when the water question became acute. Even the camels became problems, as these creatures will not let water pass their throats when it is cold. One evening, when they had been on the march for over thirteen hours, Ali declared that there was no chance of reaching the wells that night. The only water they had was about a cupful in Gertrude's flask. Then a camel-herd said that he thought there might be a water point some two hours away, so on the party went. Night fell, and still there was no sign of water; and, as there was a good chance of getting lost, they all settled down where they were in the deathly cold of the desert. Gertrude shared her ration of water with Ali and the faithful Fattuh, and waited shivering for daylight. The animals could make no complaint, but they were the worst sufferers. As soon as the grey dawn began to creep over the barren landscape, they set out again, but it took them six hours to find water in any quantity. When Ali had satisfied his thirst, he looked meditatively at Gertrude and said:

"Where is thy face in Damascus, O lady, and where thy face now?"

Gertrude whipped out her pocket mirror and looked

helplessly at the havoc which the desert wind had played with her complexion.

But even under such trying conditions, she never lost her instinctive love for this desolate country:

"We were off at five this morning in bitter frost," she wrote to her step-mother. "Can you picture the singular beauty of these moonlit departures! the frail Arab tents falling one by one, leaving the camp fires blazing into the night; the dark masses of kneeling camels; the shrouded figures binding up the loads, shaking the ice from the water skins, or crouched over the hearth for a moment's warmth before mounting. . . . So we set out across the dim wilderness. The sky ahead reddens, and fades, the moon pales and in sudden splendour the sun rushes up over the rim of the world. To see with the eyes is good, but while I wonder and rejoice to look upon this primeval existence, it does not seem to be a new thing; it is familiar, it is part of inherited memory. After an hour and a half marching we came to the pool of Khafiyeh and since there is no water for three days ahead we had to fill our empty skins. But the pool was a sheet of ice, the water skins were frozen and needed careful handling—for if you unfold them they crack and break—and we lighted a fire and set to work to thaw them out ourselves . . . But about midday the wind shifted round to the south and we began to feel the warmth of the sun. For the first time we shed our fur coats, and the lizards came out of their holes. Also the horizon was decorated with fantastic mirage which greatly added to the enjoyment of looking for ghazus. An almost imperceptible rise in the ground would from afar stand up above the solid earth as if it were the back of a camel. We saw tents with men beside them pitched on the edge of mirage lakes and when at last we did come to a stretch of shallow water, it was a long time before I could believe that it was not imaginary. I saw how the atmospheric delusion worked by watching some gazelles. They galloped away over the plain just like ordinary gazelles, but when they came to the mirage they suddenly got up on stilts and looked the size of camels. It is excessively bewildering to be deprived of the use of one's eyes in this way . . ."

In addition to the discomfort from cold the caravan was in a district notorious for its bandits, and Ali, always on the alert for ghazu raids, would parade round the camp at night, yelling:

"We are soldiers, English soldiers!"

But the raiders were keeping warm elsewhere and there was no one to hear this unexpected news!

If there were no ghazus, there were other trouble-makers who saw in the white woman's caravan a fine opportunity for loot. Local rascals used to appear and, picking quarrels with the muleteers, try to steal saddlery and arms. Gertrude usually took no notice of these disturbances, but one afternoon when Fattuh had gone to an Arab settlement to market, the sounds of an altercation so got on her nerves, when she was trying to sleep, that she leapt from her camp bed and, rushing heedlessly into the fray, routed fifteen young ruffians. After that the marauders kept clear of the camp when they knew that the Effendim was about.

And so the journey continued, every day bringing fresh adventures, fresh experiences, fresh discoveries of ruins and ancient roads, while Gertrude charted and recorded the caravan tracks and the water points until finally the Syrian Desert was conquered and the party reached Hit, which Gertrude had passed through in 1909.

Little remained of Hit but a great mound, under which lay cities dating back at least six thousand years, and all around it pitch bubbling out of the earth. Gertrude was too tired to do any excavating although she noted that the Arabs collected the pitch crust for fuel as their predecessors had done throughout the ages. Hit could wait, she pondered sleepily, but without realizing that six years later this mound would become as familiar to her as the rock garden at Rounton.

The course was now set towards Mesopotamia. Gertrude passed through Ukhaidir again and checked some of her data about the castle. She camped beneath the Tower of Babel, once part of an immense Babylonian temple dedicated to the seven spheres of heaven, and at the end of two months trekking by compass struck the first road since leaving Damascus. As they found themselves no longer dependent on their sense of direction, Fattuh exclaimed:

"WE are, praise be to God, skilled in travel—God made us."

Eventually, in the middle of March 1911, Gertrude had her first glimpse of the minarets of Baghdad glittering in the morning sunlight. The four-thousand-year-old city of Mesopotamia, the once golden home of Haroun al Raschid and Scheherazade, the town known to the Arabs as "the abode of peace," seemed to beckon mysteriously to her. The desert breeze dropped and the tall palm trees lifted their feathery heads in silence. Since the days when Hulaker, the Mongol, began to devastate Mesopotamia in the thirteenth century, Baghdad had lost her glory. Mongols and Persians and Turks had made her their vassal and she had barely remained a town of commercial importance; but today, leading a motley caravan, came a woman who was to reinstate Baghdad in its position of past glory and make it the capital of an independent Arab State. For a moment Gertrude paused outside the ancient walls, pervaded by a kind of premonition of the days when Baghdad would become her only home and, later, her eternal resting place. Then, quickly returning to a sense of reality, to the necessity of a properly cooked meal and a bath, she passed through one of the gates and was prosaically received by the Resident, Mr. Lorimer.

The moment that Gertrude relaxed she found that she was tired and she remained for a few days with her host and his wife, making only a few minor excursions and answering innumerable questions about the desert. The Resident was tremendously interested in all Gertrude had to tell and wrote a confidential letter to London in which he stated that, in all his experience of the East, he had never met an Occidental, male or female, who had such an intimate knowledge of native matters or had such complete confidence of the inhabitants.

As soon as Gertrude felt herself sufficiently rested, she said goodbye to Baghdad without any feeling of finality and turned her caravan towards the coast. Her course skirted the mountain ranges of Persia, majestic and lovely in their mantles of snow. Lovelier still to Gertrude, for those hills looked down over the country which rolled out to Tehran and its rose-scented gardens, the setting of her great happiness.

The journey to Aleppo was comparatively simple after the Syrian Desert, although the caravan had one or two hairbreadth escapes when crossing the Tigris in flood. There was, however, one incident of great significance, although hardly recorded in Gertrude's journal.

Hearing that Doctor Hogarth was excavating near Carchemish, Gertrude decided to make a detour so that she could pay him a friendly call and discuss some of her findings with him. She did not see Hogarth, but she met, for the first time, a man with whose destiny she was linked.

The excavator in charge of the Carchemish diggings was T. E. Lawrence, one day to be the conqueror of Arabia.

It was a curious encounter. Lawrence, almost exactly twenty years Gertrude's junior, wiry, undersized, a hard-working Oxford undergraduate to whom archaeology was an enthralling adventure, but without any definite ideas as to how he would steer the course of his life. Gertrude, now in her early forties, tall, good-looking, a woman of the world who had already accomplished more than most human beings in a lifetime and yet had the most important part of her career before her.

Gertrude introduced herself to Lawrence who rather shyly greeted her and offered her the simple hospitality of an excavator's camp. They spent the day discussing the country—which they would one day virtually rule—from a purely archaeological point of view, Lawrence thinking that here was a woman who seemed to have chosen a sensible kind of life without becoming domineeringly masculine, Gertrude deciding that Lawrence had the eyes of someone who one day might do things and appreciating the fact that he took his vacation with Doctor Hogarth. Neither of them had any vision of a sphinx-faced little man in abba and shesh, riding across the desert on a white, disdainful camel with a tall, handsome king-to-be at his side and a hundred thousand fierce-faced Bedouins sweeping along behind him. Or of a beautiful woman with determined eyes deciding the destiny of an ancient kingdom and placing this companion of the conqueror of the desert on the throne. They were simply two intelligent Britons with interests in common. As the little caravan disappeared in the haze of the desert, Lawrence returned to his digging, making a mental note of the name of the woman who had visited him so that he might call on her when he reached home. Gertrude had already forgotten about her young host and was urging on her caravan so that it would reach Aleppo in time for her to catch the boat to England.

CHAPTER X

Gertrude's journey across the Syrian Desert, though placing her within the ranks of famous desert travellers, was still part of the prelude to the important portion of her life. This prelude had admittedly been well filled, but except for her contributions to archaeology and the notes on the districts which she had visited, which the Geographical Society and the War Office had filed, she was little known outside her group of personal friends and those professionally interested in her activities. She had experienced sorrow, she had had adventures, there was material in her letters for a series of travel books and the volumes which she had published would have justified her settling down to watch others assume responsibilities. It seems as if she felt this, as, for two years, she made no journeys of any importance. Then, one day, was born the daring project which she had conceived years before. The historic expedition to Hayil.

Up to that time Gertrude had penetrated among unknown tribes, she had surveyed desert tracks and discovered new ruins, but others had preceded her. The journey to Hayil placed her in the category of world pioneers and, if she had achieved nothing else, this would be recorded as an adventure worthy of the most renowned builders of the British Empire.

Writing of the journey to Hayil, Doctor Hogarth says:

"Her journey was a pioneer venture which not only put on the map a line of wells, before unplaced and unknown, but also cast new light on the history of the Syrian Desert frontiers under Roman, Palmyrene and Ummayad domination. But perhaps the most valuable result consists in the mass of information that she accumulated about the tribal elements ranging between the Hejaz railway on the one bank, and the Sirhan and Nefud on the other, particularly about the Howaitat group, of which Lawrence, relying on her reports, made signal use in the Arab campaign of 1917 and 1918.

"Her stay in Hayil was fruitful of political information especially concerning both the recent history and the actual state of the Rashid House, and also its actual and probable relations with the rival power of the Ibn Sauds. Her information proved of great value during the war, when Hayil had ranged itself with the enemy and was menacing our Euphratian flank. Miss Bell became from 1915 onwards, the interpreter of all reports received from Central Arabia . . .

"To another European woman, the days before desert motor services had been thought of, such a journey would have seemed adventurous enough. But to Miss Bell, who had been into Nejd, the crossing of the Hamad seemed something of an anticlimax. Miss Bell writing in 1914 had no suspicions that, in a little more than a year, the knowledge and experience acquired during the past four months would become of national value. Nor could she foresee that, even after the war, Northern Nejd would return to the obscurity from which she had rescued it. Up to this year [1927] her visit to Hayil remains the last that has been put on scientific record . . ."

To those not familiar with the deserts of Arabia a picture of this journey to Hayil is hard to visualize. The map will suggest tracts of uninhabited land and desolate areas but not the lonely isolation. The actual miles covered by Gertrude and her caravan would mean little to a motorist on a paved road in Europe; the silence, nothing to a man in Arizona who can always find someone who speaks the same language.

The great wastes of stones, the rolling sands, the complete lack of habitations, are difficult to imagine. The Arabs, hostile to any non-Mohammedan encroachment, hating even neighbouring tribes and ready to plunder at the least excuse, the lack of water, the lack of ordinary Western commodities of life, the lack of intercourse with white people, are difficult to picture in a mind accustomed to a normal kind of existence.

Starting out on a journey of this kind might be compared to attempting to sail across the Atlantic in a small boat—with this difference, that if the weather were smooth the trip would be comparatively easy. Embarking on the desert, the weather would be only a minor consideration. Quite apart from the vital question of water, there would be that of the attitude of the nomad tribes, the problematical fidelity of one's followers, the likelihood of the camels bearing up, of death in a sandstorm. To the tourist who gazes out over the desert to see an orange moonrise or a golden sunset, it is all romance, but to one who has faced the Sirocco and the drought and the flood it is something as frightening as a tempest at sea without the reassurance of a radio station to pick up an SOS.

An expedition of Gertrude without interference by Turkish officials would have been abnormal and on this occasion, as previously, the trouble began before the caravan had been long on its way. The authorities of the Turkish government seemed to be obstinately opposed to any Occidental, and especially Gertrude, penetrating into the interior of Arabia.

Although bad weather caused a certain amount of delay and Fattuh had to be left behind, as he contracted typhoid just before the date set for the departure of the caravan, the journey began fairly successfully. This caravan was much more elaborate than any which Gertrude had assembled previously. It consisted of seventeen camels and their camelherds, eight mules and their muleteers, and riding horses. In addition to the tents and baggage for herself and her followers, who included Ali Mausar (the postman guide of the 1911 expedition) and a special guide for the Hayil district called Mohammed, there were bundles of presents for sheiks who might be encountered on the road, and provisions for four months. Gertrude's methodical mind is revealed in a letter to her father written just before her departure which goes into all the expenses connected with the trip; these total up to a little over six hundred pounds.

After squabbling with the Turks and cursing the weather and putting Fattuh in a hospital, Gertrude finally set out from Damascus on December 16, 1913, and struck southeast into the desert towards the Djebel Druze. The first twenty-four hours of travelling confirmed her appreciation of the value of Fattuh. With the exception of Ali, who was just a guide, there was not one member of the caravan who had ever travelled with a European and understood how to manipulate an English tent or prepare an Occidental meal. Whereas Gertrude usually struck camp in a period of minutes, her start on the second day out took over two hours. But she knew her Orientals now and the futility of getting impatient or raising the voice, and in a few days she had taught her followers to be almost as efficient as Fattuh.

Gertrude had dropped back into the atmosphere of the desert as if she had never belonged anywhere else.

A week later she knew that she was in the desert in earnest. The caravan was approaching a Bedouin camp when suddenly a horseman detached himself from the tents and came galloping towards the party, firing his rifle. Covering Gertrude and her two guides, the man demanded their cloaks and their arms, and before the camel-herds and muleteers could decide whether the wisest policy was to give in or fight, a host of tribesmen came pouring out of the camp, firing as they rode. One giant of a man drew a scimitar and struck the neck of Gertrude's camel to make it kneel down. Things were beginning to look black when two tribal sheiks came leisurely to join in the looting. The moment they were close to the caravan, however, they recognized Ali, and the threats became apologies and kisses and the party was taken over to the camp and treated to coffee.

When she moved on, Gertrude took one of the Bedouins with her to parley with any other bellicose tribesmen she might encounter in the neighbourhood.

It was now bitterly cold with a merciless wind hissing over the stony wastes. Gertrude spent Christmas Day with one of the great nomad chiefs of the district and gave him a cloak, while he offered her Christmas dinner, consisting of the inevitable sheep roast whole, which they ate under a frosty moon. After dinner the retainers drew near the fire and, late into the night, told stories of raiding and desert adventures.

Gertrude had often sung "While shepherds watched their flocks by night" in her home church, in a setting of snow and Christmas trees, but she had never thought how unromantic and uncomfortable the birth night of Jesus must really have been.

New Year's Day of 1914 passed practically unnoticed and on January 9th the progress of the caravan was brought to a forced halt.

Gertrude had told Fattuh to come down by train to a station on the Mecca railway as soon as he was fit, from there he would have to find his way and pick up the caravan as soon as possible. As the days passed and Fattuh did not put in an appearance, Gertrude began to worry. Her staff was working as well as could be expected, but it was not the same as having Fattuh and she felt that all the months in unknown Arabia without him would be impossible. She accordingly headed her caravan in a westerly direction to within sight of Siza on the railway. She found Fattuh, who had just arrived, pale and thin, but eager to be back with his mistress; she found a large mail and she also found a Turkish officer and ten soldiers who told her that they had been hunting her ever since she had left Damascus. The officer was angry and insolent but Gertrude, remembering the ways of Orientals, said nothing. Even when he ransacked the baggage, confiscated the arms and finally arrested Fattuh, Gertrude never made the smallest comment. This icy demeanour eventually worried the Turk, and he came to Gertrude, first condescendingly, then conciliatingly and finally apologetically, asking if he could do anything for her. Gertrude replied that he could do nothing until he appeared before a court of justice in Damascus, as she was returning there at once to report the looting of her camp, her detention, and the unlawful arrest of her servant. The officer turned pale, became confused and hurriedly left, only to come back a little later to say that he had consulted the "authorities" and found that there had been some sort of misunderstanding. Gertrude still made no comment, until the man, now abject and humble, returned her arms and Fattuh and implored her to go where and when she pleased. Without further ado, Gertrude ordered the camp to be broken; and, still saying nothing to the officer, she set her course south towards the merciless and practically unknown wastes of the Nefud wilderness.

For the first time in its history a white woman was penetrating into the Great Arabian Desert.

It was a country of flints and dust with here and there sparse scrub. The sun blazed down making the land to shimmer and mirages to spring up and vanish as the caravan approached. Silence and loneliness wrapped themselves about the little party like an impenetrable veil. Even the Damascene members of the caravan seemed to suffer from the oppressive solitude, for after a few days of this monotonous trekking three of them threw down their camel sticks and refused to go any further. Luckily there was a Bedouin settlement near by and Mohammed was able to find substitutes for the mutineers.

Water became more and more scarce. A very occasional well, usually a brackish pool. Gertrude and her followers relied on what was carried in the skins and the animals did as best they could. A dry and barren world, an explanation why the Mohammedan idea of Paradise is a country of grassy fields, evergreen trees and rivers of cool water.

The guides did not like approaching camps for fear of being raided, but when four days had passed without a sign of water Gertrude decided that a risk must be taken. They were now in the pasturing area of the famous Howaitat nomads, a proud, warlike people renowned for their bravery. When, therefore, a spiral column of smoke was seen rising from the desert, Gertrude led her caravan towards it. A magnificent person on a richly saddled horse who bore himself with regal dignity came out to meet the weary party. Gertrude, with her hand on a cocked pistol beneath her coat, greeted the man who at once smiled. It was Mohammed Abu Tayyi, the paramount Sheik of the Howaitat, whose journeys had taken him into the districts where Gertrude was known. The chieftain went through the solemn Arab greetings of people of equal rank and begged Gertrude to be his guest; and, trying to use the proper expressions in addressing one so noble, she accepted.

"Of an evening we sat in his big tent," she wrote, "and I listened to the tales and the songs of the desert, the exploits of Audah, who is one of the most famous raiders of these days, and romantic adventures of the princes of Nejd. Mohammed sat beside me on the rugs which were spread upon the clean soft sand, his great figure wrapped in a sheepskin cloak, and sometimes he puffed at his narghile and listened to the talk and sometimes he joined in, his black eyes flashing in question and answer. I watched it all and found much to look at. And then, long after dark, the nagas, the camel mothers, would come home with their calves and crouch down in the sand outside the open tent. Mohammed got up, drew his robes about him, and went out into the night with a huge wooden bowl, which he brought back to me full to the brim of camel's milk. And I fancy that when you have drunk the milk of the naga over the camp fire of Abu Tayyi you are baptised of the desert and there is no other salvation for you."

This was the first and only meeting of Gertrude and Abu Tayyi, but three years later this chance encounter was to greatly serve Lawrence when he was fighting his way through the Howaitat tribal areas.

Gertrude remained for a while with the Howaitat, resting the animals and taking in supplies of water. When she was ready to start, she asked the sheik for a guide. But as soon as she mentioned the route she wished to follow, there was a silence and queer looks exchanged among the Arabs. The sheik shook his head. No man could go by that route, it was an "empty" desert, the only people who ever crossed it were raiders, the Effendim must not entertain such a project. Gertrude insisted and pleaded but there was nothing which would change the opinion of her Arab hosts. Finally she had to compromise and make for her destination by a longer way. The decision was wise for she passed through a country which was comparatively fertile and the camels were able to take in a store of food against the more difficult part of the journey to come. Even by this route, things did not run smoothly.

Coming within sight of another camp Gertrude decided that it would be safer to go to it than let the owners come after her. She accordingly approached and was received with courtesy; but it was only pretence, for no sooner had the camels been unloaded than a one-eyed ruffian appeared and declared that no Christian had ever visited this part of the country and none should leave to tell the tale. He then proposed to Fattuh and Mohammed that they should kill the infidel and share the spoil! Getting no encouragement from these two, he tried the others, and disgusted at the unbelievable loyalty of these Arabs to a white woman he started going through the packs of the caravan. In spite of being rather afraid Gertrude maintained that disdainful calm which always made troublesome Orientals feel ill at ease. It was more difficult this time as she knew that she was at the mercy of this bandit, but after a while the man could no longer stand the white woman's silent disapproval; and after requesting a "present" of her Zeiss glasses and a revolver he became quite affable and supplied the caravan with a guide.

The caravan reached the edge of the Nefud, the great Arabian sand desert, on February 12. As Gertrude caught sight of the golden dunes stretching away till they merged with the sky she stopped, holding her breath, overwhelmed with admiration and amazement.

Away, away into an infinite distance, thousands of square miles of sand which a caravan, moving at a normal pace, would take weeks to cross. Thousands of square miles of sand without a vestige of water, with no vegetation excepting that which springs up after a rainstorm and as quickly dies. The land of thirst and the sandstorm, the land of silence broken by the voice of no bird, of no beast.

The sand dunes of this part of the desert roll out towards the horizon like the waves of the Atlantic on a stormy day, making depressions hundreds of feet deep in which a caravan could be lost to sight from another caravan only a short distance away. The wind is always blowing over the dunes, making their crests to resemble breakers chasing each other to the shore and changing their conformation. And like the sea the dunes move and overwhelm all that stands in their path. There is a desolate majesty about the sand desert which is more inspiring than any of the great oceans.

Gertrude did not move for a while and sat on her camel watching the rich colouring of the sand as the sun changed the dunes from yellow to orange and from orange to red. Then bringing herself back to reality, she urged her camel forward and set out on the gleaming, virgin sand. She did not attempt to traverse the whole desert, but cut across its northwest corner, taking about five days to do it. She knew that her guides were experienced and trustworthy, but she felt as if she were wandering through a labyrinth, winding round deep sand pits sometimes half a mile long with banks too steep to climb. As the crow flies the caravan rarely made more than a mile to the hour, but the effort was more exhausting than a day's march along a road. However, only one of the camels fell by the wayside, which Fattuh despatched with his long knife, crying as he did so: "In the name of God, God is most powerful!" and abandoned it to be covered and preserved by the ever-drifting sand.

Four years later Lawrence of Arabia was to pass near this part of the desert with his Arab levies and, later, wrote in his *Seven Pillars of Wisdom:* [1]

> ". . . Accordingly, we inclined right, over flats of limestone and sand, and saw a distant corner of the Great Nefud, the famous belts of the sand dune which cut off Jebel Shammar from the Syrian Desert. Palgrave, the Blunts and Gertrude Bell, amongst the storied travellers, had crossed it, and I begged Auda to bear off a little and let us enter it and their company: but he growled that men went to the Nefud only of necessity, and that the son of his father did not raid on a tottering camel. Our business was to reach Arfaja alive . . ."

As dawn broke on February 17, Gertrude reached the

[1] From "Seven Pillars of Wisdom," by T. E. Lawrence, copyright, 1926, 1935, by Doubleday, Doran and Company, Inc.

barren sandstone crags of the Djebel Misma, which bound the Nefud to the east, and passed beyond them into Nejd. Behind her lay the nightmare of drifting sand, but it looked inviting in comparison to the terrifying landscape which she now saw in the growing light. Rocks blackened by prehistoric fire dropped steeply into a wilderness of jagged peaks set in a bed of hard sand with, beyond, a vacant plain stretching out interminably, untilled and unpeopled and scattered over with isolated tables and towers of sandstone. It was the most frighteningly dead and empty country on which she had ever looked.

The marching was, however, much easier, and plenty of water from rainstorms was found in sandstone hollows. Still, it was not the kind of place where anyone would wish to linger, water or no water, so Gertrude hurried on the caravan until it came again to inhabited territories with small settlements, which looked like English villages to the parched eyes of the daughter of the Yorkshire moors. The worst of the journey was over and the little party travelled more leisurely until, on the twenty-fourth of February, the mysterious city of Hayil came into view.

Gertrude was not too certain how she would be received, so she pitched her camp a few miles away from the battlemented walls of the town and sent Mohammed and Ali to announce her arrival.

The next morning she marched against Hayil. As she approached the outer keep she saw Ali coming towards her accompanied by three horsemen carrying lances. He greeted her and hurriedly told her that the Emir Ibn Rashid was away on a raiding expedition but that his uncle Ibrahim, who had been left in charge of the town, was ready to welcome her. The tone in which Ali spoke made Gertrude look up at him questioningly, but before he could say anything further they were at the entrance of the city and being received by a sinister-looking Arab who waited there with Mohammed. Gertrude returned the salutation, feeling peculiarly ill at ease, and passed through the great portal; the gates clashed menacingly behind her. She was then relieved of her horse and walked up a huge sloping passageway into an open court and on into a vast pillared reception room where she waited with the slaves.

These slaves, Ali explained to her in whispers, had a curious position in Hayil and were regarded as part of the family of the ruling dynasty to the extent of being put to death when, as often happened, an Emir was summarily deposed by a rival.

Gertrude waited with these slaves, who did not seem in the least interested in her and lounged about the dimly lighted hall. She was becoming restless and vaguely apprehensive when a curtain was drawn aside and two women appeared. The first was elderly and apparently a kind of housekeeper called Lu-lu-ah, the other a lovely young Circassian who introduced herself as Turkiyyeh. Turkiyyeh was the favourite of the Emir and had been sent to him as a gift by the Sultan himself. Gertrude took to Turkiyyeh at once and Turkiyyeh to Gertrude and, in a few minutes, the Circassian was chattering away and asking questions about the world she used to know as if she and the English-woman came from the same village. A rather unappetizing collation was served, after which the two ladies retired announcing to Gertrude that her host would now honour her with his presence.

In a few moments Ibrahim came in wearing magnificent robes of Indian silk and girt with a gold-mounted sword. A huge retinue of slaves preceded and followed him in stately procession. He bowed to Gertrude and they exchanged the long Arab courtesies, talked banalities for a moment and the interview was over. Just as he was leaving, Ibrahim stared searchingly at Gertrude and said that, in view of the fact that the Emir was away, it would be better if she did not leave the house where she was now staying. The remark was made politely and apparently innocent of guile, but as the heavy curtains fell softly behind Ibrahim's escort Gertrude had an uneasy feeling that she was a prisoner in the great palace. For the moment this did not worry her as she was worn out after her long journey, and the camels would require a few days on the local pastures before continuing the journey to the north.

But when a few days had passed and Gertrude's energy had returned, she became fidgety. Turkiyyeh visited her daily and was charming and chatty but always evaded the point when any question of going out or leaving was brought up. So Gertrude observed her studied patience and wrote letters and mended her clothes. Ali and Mohammed came to see her at regular intervals and Fattuh was in constant attendance, but they also could tell her nothing concerning her detention. Then, one morning, she decided to return Ibrahim's call. The request was immediately granted and that night she was led by slaves through the silent, empty streets of the great city to the fortress palace of the Emir. It was an eerie experience, a feeling of being utterly alone in the midst of a host of murderous people who had little respect for human life in general and none whatever for

Gertrude's. Troops in mediaeval armour met her at the gate of the palace and led her through dimly lighted courtyards to the reception room. She found Ibrahim seated with a crowd of notables in a huge pillared chamber. Everyone rose at her entrance and sat down again when she did. Generalities were talked for an hour, but when Gertrude broached the subject of leaving Hayil the slaves brought censers and swung them three times, denoting that the interview was over, and she was escorted back to her "prison" and left.

Gertrude was now in a quandary. It was definitely evident that she was being detained, and although she felt that escape might be possible there was another difficulty. She had no more money. Before leaving Damascus she had deposited two hundred pounds with the Emir's agent in Syria with instructions to send the necessary credit to Hayil, but whenever she asked about this she was informed that nothing could be done as long as the Emir was away. The date of his return was regarded as problematical; it might be in a week, perhaps in a month, possibly in two!

Not one word of all this did Gertrude believe, so she sent for Ali and Mohammed and made a plan. They were to sell some of the camels and they would get away as best they could and hope that the funds would last until they reached some place where their credit was good. Mohammed carried out these orders and brought the money to Gertrude. When, however, the details of the escape came to be discussed, Ali, who had two uncles living in Hayil, shook his head. He had not liked to mention the matter before, but all these projects were suspected; and even if the Effendim made a success of leaving the town, which was not likely, she would certainly be caught and brought back.

Gertrude became angry and inquired who was at the bottom of all this nonsense. Lowering his voice, Ali whispered that it was the Emir's aunt, Fatima, who was actually in possession of the two hundred pounds. Gertrude became more and more annoyed and demanded a further interview with Ibrahim.

Once more the same reception and the same cordialities, once more Ibrahim evaded the issue while Gertrude pressed for an answer. It was like Moses pleading for the Israelites before Pharaoh in an atmosphere of Baghdad under Haroun al Raschid. But Gertrude had none of Moses' plagues to offer and little of his patience, and she refused to take "No" for an answer. Finally, Ibrahim began to weaken before this determined English-woman and, in order to pacify her, said that of course she should go, of course she should have her money, there had never been any question about the matter—"good night!"

Gertrude returned to her quarters in triumph and confided to Turkiyyeh that she had got the better of old Ibrahim. Turkiyyeh listened, smiled in a way which left Gertrude uneasy again, and retired.

In the morning Gertrude demanded that her men and her horses and camels be sent round to her quarters, but after a long delay word was brought that they could not be found. She was now getting frantic, almost foreseeing being left to languish for ever in Hayil. She knew, moreover, that she had set out on this trip against the advice of the authorities and could expect little help from that direction.

She was still fuming and wondering what she should do

next when Saiyid, the chief eunuch and the most powerful man in Hayil, called on her and, without preliminaries, said bluntly that Gertrude could not leave until the Emir returned and that it was no good making a fuss about it. He then bowed himself superbly out of the apartment.

Gertrude sank back on her brocaded cushions, perplexed. Eunuchs, Emirs, Nubian slaves . . . No, it was impossible, this was the twentieth century . . . She rubbed her eyes expecting to find herself awake again in normal surroundings. But instead there was a bowing retainer bidding her to a feast offered by Mudi, the mother of the Emir.

Gertrude got up resignedly and followed the slave, with a helpless feeling that she had somehow strayed back into a tenth century Asia and had no knowledge of how to find her way forward again into her own age.

She found Turkiyyeh, lovely as a young Scheherazade, waiting for her. The other guests were all women dressed in flowery silks and glittering with jewels, with a sprinkling of children in the costumes of grown-ups. Blue sensuous incense drifted about the high-ceilinged room, while the hostess and her friends sat on rich carpets nibbling sweetmeats and sipping thick coffee which impassive eunuchs handed round. The conversation was about matters feminine, but with that Asiatic restraint of another era.

Gertrude said little, overcome by the unbelievable atmosphere, expecting any moment to find her rough travelling dress changed into a ruby-studded robe and hear her name called to join some adoring young Sultan. Where were Rounton and the rock garden and her father and the Yorkshire miners? What had become of her friends in Paris and London? Did they really exist or had all that life been a fantasy of her mind? . . . The party quietly broke up and slaves with lances escorted the lone and extremely perturbed English-woman back to her apartments.

The next day Gertrude decided that tenth century or no tenth century she was still Miss Bell and when Turkiyyeh came to visit her she spoke to her as one girl to another. No Oriental polite phrases, just a woman who wanted a friend's help. Turkiyyeh at once responded and, discarding the rôle of a Circassian princess, promised that she would see what she could do.

Nothing happened immediately, but a few days later Gertrude was invited to visit the Emir's gardens. She found all the royal babies who had not been murdered by the last usurping Emir, two young sheiks, various court dignitaries and Saiyid, the chief eunuch. They sat on carpets in a peacock blue pavilion, which might have come straight out of a Persian miniature. They wandered through lovely grounds, planted with fruit-laden trees, to the tinkle of sparkling fountains, while the little children walked solemnly hand in hand in their robes of brocades. Gertrude asked the usual questions of Saiyid, but he only smiled and offered more coffee. Then, suddenly, she lost her temper and spoke to the chief eunuch without the usual Eastern paraphrases. When she had finished her tirade she turned her back and left the men sitting—a gesture only used by great sheiks—and found her way back to her quarters alone.

Gertrude felt better, but as her rage cooled she realized that she had broken the strictest rules of etiquette and could expect no favours; there would probably be reprisals from one so powerful and proud as Saiyid. She hoped that Turkiyyeh would come and keep her company, but as it grew late and she was deciding to go to bed the chief eunuch entered her apartments with two other men. Gertrude braced herself, holding her pistol cocked in her pocket, but instead of hearing a doom pronounced, Saiyid, after the politest preliminary speech, announced that Gertrude was free to leave when she pleased, in token of which he had brought a bag containing the two hundred pounds which had inadvertently been mislaid. He then made a deep obeisance and disappeared, leaving Gertrude speechless. Her first reaction was that this was all a trick of the nature of Pharaoh and the Israelites. However, early next morning Turkiyyeh came to the apartment and said that she had taken up the matter with Fatima, pointed out that this way of treating a distinguished Occidental guest was disgraceful, and so persuaded her that when the chief eunuch came fuming in after being insulted by Gertrude he was curtly told to give her her money and let her go.

On March 20, nearly one month after sighting the battlemented walls of Hayil, Gertrude with her full caravan left this city of the Arabian Nights and, after kissing Turkiyyeh who sobbed like a child, set her course north towards Baghdad.

The remainder of the journey was difficult and interesting, but rather an anticlimax after the sand desert of Nefud and the mediaeval happenings in Hayil.

From a point of view of raids the caravan had more trouble during this portion of the trip than before. Luckily Mohammed had found a friend of the powerful Ghazalat tribe to accompany him. Soon after leaving Hayil the caravan was attacked by hordes of Madan Bedouins, the most notorious raiders of this part of the desert. The presence of the Ghazalat tribesman caused a halt in the looting while the chief of the Madans tried to come to some agreement with him. The Ghazalat, however, was loyal to his friend Mohammed and the raiders had to let the caravan go on its way, not wishing to create a feud with a tribe which was much stronger than their own. The next day the caravan was again attacked with the same procedure and results.

Gertrude had become apathetic to everything and rode along leaving the settling of these commotions to Ali and Mohammed. The strain of uncertainty in Hayil had worn her down and she wanted a little peaceful relaxation and above all a change of clothes and a proper bath. All the magnificence of the Emir's palaces, the rich foods, the brocades and jewels, were as in all Oriental establishments façades concealing filth and squalor. The sweetmeats to take away the taste of rancid butter, the incense to dispel unmentionable odours, the heavy perfumes to disguise unwashed bodies. During her enforced stay in Hayil Gertrude would have given all the precious stones about her for one really good bath.

At last, on March 29, she caught sight of the golden minarets of the Kuzeman mosque sending her a glittering welcome from Baghdad. Arabs, deserts, ruins, were quickly forgotten and she sank to rest in what seemed to her the most advanced kind of civilization. The city, which was one day to claim her mortal remains, gently nursed her back to health.

When Gertrude started again, it was up the valley of the Euphrates and thence across the Syrian Desert—a mere stroll in the country compared with what she had lately accomplished—until she eventually pitched her camp where, five months previously, she had mounted her camel to ride out of Damascus for Hayil.

This, unsuspected by her, was the last journey she was to make in the desert of Arabia with her caravan. It was the end of May 1914 and she was to find herself too occupied to undertake any expeditions until the events brought about by the Great War were to call her to duties in which her experiences in the East would be used to their fullest extent.

Not in the least conceited about her achievements, regarding them almost as journeys unworthy of being recorded, Gertrude nevertheless held a unique position among the world's explorers. Doughty and Burton had done much to clear up many mysteries concerning the deserts of Arabia, but their work, other than from a literary point of view, was never put to practical use. Lawrence brought about the revolt of the Arabs in the desert, but the constructiveness of his task died with the end of the war. To Gertrude Bell it was left to create something in the Near East which still lives and will undoubtedly continue for many years to come.

She was now forty-six, and the lovely girl graduate of Oxford had developed into a handsome woman with striking personality and penetrating eyes. She had learned how to meet emergencies, how to face hardships, how to handle men, but she was entirely feminine. Her name was known from the Red Sea to the Persian Gulf, her friends numbered Persians and Syrians and Arabs, but her own people still regarded her as the daughter of Sir Hugh Bell. To Gertrude herself she was a nobody who had had an interesting life because she had had the means to do what she wanted. Even when her name was becoming "news" and the public wanted to know about her, she avoided interviews with reporters and begged her father not to allow her picture to appear in the press. And when the Royal Geographical Society awarded her its medal, she commented: "It was an absurd thing to give me; they must have been hard up for travellers this year."

It is unlikely that there has ever been a great historical figure who had less to say for herself than Gertrude Bell.

PART III

WAR

CHAPTER XI

THE OUTBREAK OF WAR in 1914 found every country in Europe, except one, caught unawares. The least prepared of all was Great Britain and her imperial satellites.

The British army was literally the smallest in the world, and there had been little thought of its employment in any major capacity on the Continent of Europe. Not only was this army shipped overseas, but it began to grow like some fabulous monster, so that the organizations connected with the huge body of men found difficulty in keeping pace with the expansion. It was in situations of this kind that Gertrude could be at her best.

After the outbreak of hostilities she moved about Yorkshire, addressing miners and rousing the people to put the whole of their energies into bringing victory for England and her allies. Then, for a while, she did some nursing at Lord Onslow's hospital at Clandon. This was not, however, the type of work for which she was in any way suited and she was glad when Lord Robert Cecil asked her to go to Boulogne and take up an executive post in the lately set up offices for tracing the wounded and the missing.

When Gertrude arrived at the headquarters of this new organization she found the whole place in an unspeakable muddle, no one seemed to be in charge, no one seemed to have any idea of how to set about tackling this complicated task. Gertrude smiled—compared to her jaunts in the Syrian Desert this would be child's play—and, rolling up her sleeves, she set to work.

Physical exhaustion, privations and treacherous weather meant nothing out of the normal to Gertrude. She had a persevering capacity to stick to anything which she undertook until it was finished. By keeping her staff working with her literally day and night, she had the office in Boulogne organized in an incredibly short time and a new office opened in Rouen. No sooner was this done than Lord Robert Cecil recalled her to London to get the main office of the similar unit out of chaos. This she did with the same efficiency.

The war had now been going on for a year. The German onslaughts had been checked and the four great armies had dug themselves in from the English Channel to the Alps. It was evident that Kitchener's slogan (at first ridiculed), "for three years or duration of the war," was no fantasy. Hostilities had, moreover, shifted to other parts of the world and notably to the Near East. Doctor Hogarth held a temporary commission in the Intelligence Service and worked in Cairo, and the young excavator called Lawrence, whom Gertrude had met at Carchemish in 1911, was advocating a revolt of the Arabs in the desert. In November 1915, Doctor Hogarth suddenly realized that the person who had more knowledge about the geography of uncharted Arabia and the Bedouins than anyone else in the world was missing from the General Staff in the Near East. He at once brought Gertrude's name before the authorities and was backed by an old friend of the Bells, Captain Reginald Hall, R.N.,[1]

[1] Later, Admiral Sir Reginald Hall, K.C.M.G.

who was one of his colleagues, with the result that she was summoned to Cairo.

Gertrude had officially taken her place among the builders of Britain's Empire.

As soon as she arrived in Egypt, she was put to work to fill in the gaps in the Intelligence files with her information about the desert tracks, the tribes and the characteristics of the various sheiks. This information was to be used eventually by Lawrence when he penetrated into Arabia to bring the Arabs over to the allied side and lead them against the Turks. Curiously enough, Lawrence, at this juncture, had not yet made any great impression on Gertrude. She refers to him in her letters as someone with an able mind, as a companion at dinner, as one of her colleagues, but there is nothing about his personality. Lawrence was a peculiar man and one of his peculiarities was the fact that he attracted women without being attracted himself. This magnetism does not seem to have touched Gertrude. Perhaps she had too much work to do.

As a matter of fact she did have a tremendous task to perform and one of immense responsibility. There was no one who knew the desert and its peoplc as she, and the General Staff was to depend on her for its information. But she had the ability to relax and when not drawing up reports she continued taking lessons in Arabic, though why she should need more knowledge of that language is not clear. She dined at the various staff messes, she discussed ruins with C. L. Woolley, the archaeologist and excavator, who now, like Hogarth and Lawrence, went about in uniform; she rode, and she wrote home detailed descriptions of what she was doing, interlarded with accounts of parties and requests to send out clothes suitable for going out.

By the beginning of 1916 she had sorted out her information, drawn up her report and delivered it to G.H.Q. The authorities were amazed not only at the completeness of her data and its intimate detail, but by the suggestions which were rather those of a trained Intelligence officer than a good-looking woman. The result was that a further opening for her abilities had to be found. It came from a quite unexpected direction: India.

One of the great difficulties which Britain had to contend with during the Great War was the vast and remotely separated areas which her armies had to cover. Each General Staff regarded its particular mission as the deciding factor in the hostilities and wanted every possible support from the Government, regardless of exigencies on other fronts. As a result of this attitude there was often lack of cohesion and co-operation between Commanders-in-Chief. The Indian Army was playing a big part in the war, chiefly in the Near East, but the government of India was jealous of letting troops out of its control. It was a delicate situation to broach and it was thought that the most suitable person to explain the whole situation to the Viceroy was Gertrude Bell.

The negotiations which led up to this mission were worked out unofficially. The Viceroy, Lord Hardinge, was the Charles Hardinge with whom Gertrude had taken walks in Bucharest in 1888; he had seen her since then, he was aware of her achievements and felt convinced that she would be impartial. Accordingly when the matter was taken up officially, the Viceroy immediately signified his approval and Gertrude left Egypt at a moment's notice. An officer of the Staff in Cairo said that he had never seen anyone mobilize so rapidly; but what was packing up and boarding a troopship to a person who had loaded up her home and belongings onto camels day after day in wind and rain and sandstorm!

Gertrude started off full of enthusiasm, but, by the time she had sailed down the Red Sea, crossed the Bay of Bengal and travelled over the Scinde Desert, she had begun to wonder what her mission actually was and whether the authorities really wanted to talk to her. However, her qualms were dispelled when she reached Delhi and found waiting for her the viceregal car, which took her straight to Lord Hardinge who was only too eager to hear her views on the situation. In fact she was quite overwhelmed by the attention she received and wrote to her father:

"It is interesting, deeply interesting, but oh, it is an anxious job. I wish, I wish I knew more, and was more . . . the Viceroy is anxious that I should go to Basrah and stay there with the Intelligence Service and lend a hand, but that all depends on what their views are and whether I can be of any use. That hangs on me, I feel, as we have often said, all you can do for people is to give them the opportunity of making a place for themselves . . . I think that I have pulled things straight between Delhi and Cairo. But nothing will ever keep them straight except a constant personal intercourse—it ought not to be difficult to manage and I am convinced that it is essential."

Gertrude spent almost three weeks in Delhi studying the government files on the situation in Arabia. She discussed all possible eventualities with the Intelligence Departments and at the end of February felt that she was sufficiently primed to join the expeditionary force in Mesopotamia.

On March 3, 1916, she was on Arab soil again, steaming

up the Euphrates towards Basrah. She felt elated at being once more in a country which she knew and among a people whom she understood. It was like coming home.

The Chief Political Officer (later High Commissioner) was Sir Percy Cox, Britain's most distinguished expert on the Near East, whom Gertrude had originally met in England when he was Resident in the Persian Gulf. She was at that time planning to make her journey to Hayil from one of the Arab ports of the Persian Gulf which were under Cox's jurisdiction. The project was discussed at great length but, owing to the unsettled state of the coastal tribes, was abandoned until four years later when it was carried out as already recorded.

Sir Percy was delighted to see Gertrude, whose fortunes in various parts of Arabia he had closely followed, and a deep and understanding friendship began which was to last until Gertrude's death.

Cox was a great administrator, a man of learning with an extensive knowledge of Mesopotamia and Persia, but his present task was the most difficult he had ever undertaken and it is to be wondered whether he would have achieved the same results without the devoted help of his new collaborator.

Gertrude's first days in her new post were filled with depressing feelings. She did not quite know what was expected of her, she could see no tangible results at the end of a day's work; the woman who had been accustomed to run her own life did not like being a subordinate. She sensed a suspicious attitude in the older men, especially the generals, who could not see what business a woman had in Basrah in time of war: as a nurse, well and good; but as a political officer, and one with such determined views, it seemed all wrong. The younger men knew little about her work in the East and were inclined to be condescending. Gertrude concealed her innermost feelings and, observing the same tactics as she had with the people of the desert, bided her time and said nothing.

On March 9th she was asked to lunch at Government House to meet all the generals: General Sir Percy Lake, General Cowper, General Shaw, General Money, were all present with their staff officers and A.D.C.'s. They were anxious for a "close up" of this preposterous female who wanted to tell them how to fight the Turks—why, she was worse than that crank Lawrence with his dreams about Arab irregulars creating a revolt in the desert!

Gertrude dressed herself with care; she discarded her working clothes and became cool and perfumed and feminine. She walked into Government House playing the rôle of Miss Bell of Rounton Grange paying a visit to the High Commissioner. She smiled at the pompous generals, she listened to their conversation and encouraged them to talk. She made them feel the woman in her, she flattered their military vanity and, when she had them all sitting at her feet, she started to talk. The lunch party lasted long into the afternoon. When it broke up, the generals looked at one another, made a simultaneous and ineffectual effort to see Gertrude home and separated rather stiffly.

The next morning when Gertrude arrived at the stuffy little office which had been assigned to her behind a store, she found all her things being moved. Surprised and, with a nauseating feeling that perhaps she had not been liked by the generals and was being sent home, she inquired the reason.

"Orders!"

"Whose orders?"

"Headquarters."

Gertrude went out to investigate and found that all her papers and books and maps were being taken to one of the best rooms of the General Staff, with a cool verandah and all the comforts which a woman might need. From that day Gertrude's authority was never questioned, her views were accepted and her word was law over the length and breadth of the Tigris and Euphrates valleys.

One month later Lawrence appeared at Basrah and instinctively made for Gertrude. To a month it was exactly five years since he had been prodding among the excavations at Carchemish when Gertrude passed by. It may have been the proximity of the generals, it may have been the instinct for the Arabs and the mutual love of the desert or just a man and a woman who wanted to talk, but these two suddenly discovered each other. For the whole of one day and part of the night they discussed their most intimate thoughts which included a vast scheme for the government of the universe! In the morning Gertrude saw the little man off on the boat, which was to take him up the river to the battle which was raging and to the beginning of his short-lived glory. Lawrence was still plain Mr. Lawrence to the world, to the generals a crank who had original and impractical ideas, but to Gertrude something different which she understood. She was not to see him again until after the war, as Lawrence of Arabia, one of the most talked-of men of the time, but it was on that April night of 1916 that he made the greatest impression on her.

In the meanwhile the war in Mesopotamia was not being waged very creditably by the British, and the despised Turks were proving themselves to be stout soldiers. Kut el Amarah had fallen and General Townshend and the gallant survivors of the siege had been taken into captivity for the rest of the war. The situation looked black for England and it seemed as if the Arabs might change their minds about siding with, what looked like, a lost cause. For the first time since Gertrude had joined the staff of Sir Percy Cox she came officially into action.

Ibn Raschid, of the same family as the Emir who had kept Gertrude a prisoner in Hayil and one of the most powerful desert chiefs, was not far away and to him Gertrude went. Back in the atmosphere of black tents and camels she knew what arguments to use; and when she returned to Basrah she had the word of Ibn Raschid that he would honour his pledge—which he kept until peace was signed.

She encountered also another great Arab figure, Ibn Saud, the Wahabi chieftain of Southern Nejd whose authority extended to the Persian Gulf. Ibn Saud had heard much about Gertrude in connection with her journey to Hayil, but he had never met her or, for that matter, any white woman. He held the Moslem's opinion of females and could not understand what place anyone of this sex could hold in the administration of a country. But when the introduction was made he behaved as if talking to European women was his usual occupation and, like the generals, quickly succumbed to her personality. Gertrude liked the Bedouin chief, too, and realized that he also had a personality far above that of the average sheik and might easily become a menace to Mesopotamia. This intuition was later justified when Ibn Saud took possession of Hayil and began to attack the nomads of the tribes which had sworn allegiance to the government of Faisal. Immediate reprisals were carried out from the air; but the peace which was eventually made was rather due to Gertrude persuading Ibn Saud that it would be wiser policy to remain on friendly terms with the British-protected realms of Iraq.

The reason for this critical situation in Mesopotamia was a muddling policy of the British Government. The Viceroy of India could not be held responsible as Kitchener had drained the country of regular troops and equipment, so that when things became serious in the Near East adequate assistance could not be sent out in time. Furthermore, all the best generals had gone to Gallipoli or France.

Circumstances rushed England into war in the Orient, but once there she showed a complete disregard for a comprehensive political scheme. Mesopotamia was treated as if it were an isolated unit instead of part of Arabia. There was a certain amount of excuse for this as, until 1914, little was known about the country outside a circle of archaeologists, students of ancient history and theologians interested in the Old Testament. The practical value of the oil fields which had supplied Noah with pitch for the lining of his Ark had not been considered, and an independent kingdom of Iraq had only been dreamed of by a few idealistic Arabs.

Mesopotamia might be described as the country with the oldest recorded history in the world. In an area of barely one hundred and fifty thousand square miles some of the most prominent races, with high degrees of civilization, came into being and disappeared. The Sumerians, the Hittites, the Aramaeans, the Assyrians, the Persians, the Greeks, the Parthians, dominated Mesopotamia at various times until the seventh century after Christ, when the Arabs swept in and established Islam. For a thousand years they ruled the country, when their influence was superseded by that of the Turks. This influence continued until the Great War and the entry of the Turks on the side of Germany, which led to the British campaign and the eventual creation of the Kingdom of Iraq.

But although the Turks were masters of Mesopotamia in 1914, the politics of the country were indissolubly connected with the great and far-reaching Arab question, which presents different problems as they are regarded from different angles, but remains always the same indivisible block. The co-ordinating of Arab politics should have been done by experts in England. But there was no one to do it, no one who had ever given it much thought, and it was left to the British in Egypt to thrash out, in the face of great opposition, some sort of wild scheme which eventually and chiefly by luck formed the basis of Britain's relations with the Arabs.

England has a reputation of muddling through, and undoubtedly achieves things under this banner, after wading in floods of blood and tears of humiliation. The disasters of the Mesopotamian campaign, the loss of life, the grievous aftermaths, might have been avoided had Gertrude Bell been made use of in London at the outbreak of hostilities and given a free hand.

By the end of May the generals, who had nearly had apoplexy when Gertrude came out to join the staff, were taking her with them on their trips towards the front. In

June she was officially made a member of the Indian Expeditionary Force, with pay—which amused her, though she refused to wear a uniform. She endeavoured to remain cool and feminine in the terrific heat of the Mesopotamian summer which was just beginning, and seemed to bear up better under the torrid temperature than her male colleagues. Later in the season she succumbed to the local fever, but refused to take care of herself, feeling that all the attention of the doctors and nurses should be concentrated on the wounded and sick soldiers. However, the insidious climate of the Euphrates Valley was not going to let a mere woman, even if she was Gertrude Bell, scoff at its fevers; and before long she was in the hospital with a bad case of jaundice.

The jaundice depressed Gertrude. She had never given in to illness in her life and the fact of being tied to her bed irritated her and delayed her recovery. She began to worry over the situation and became obsessed with an idea that Great Britain was going to lose the war and be forced to abandon what it held in Asia. She began to mistrust the Arabs, to distrust herself. Then, all of a sudden she was well again and all her fighting spirit and sense of humour returned. She wanted to be alive and about, and soon the gloomy forebodings had disappeared and she was writing to her step-mother:

> "Will you please send me a winter hat. Also I would immensely like a soft black satin gown which I could either wear by day or night. I would like Marthe to make it as she will make me something pretty . . ."

Eventually the parcel arrived from Marthe, but the gown had been abstracted and all that was left inside the box was a little black satin coat and a gold flower. Gertrude was almost as infuriated when she discovered the loss as if every Arab tribe had deserted the British cause.

To her father she wrote asking for books to be sent out every month, a varied assortment—a few novels, poetry and translations of Greek plays.

For the moment she had little official work to do, and she spent much of her time in seeing all the sheiks who passed through Basrah and keeping herself in touch with the Arab chiefs "upcountry." The Sheik of Khamiseyeh and Sheik Hamud of the Dhafir welcomed her as an old friend and she introduced them to the general in command and acted as interpreter.

She spent the third Christmas of the war doing a little excavating near the tomb reputed to be that of Ezra and was thankful to be escaping the seasonal rejoicings at British Headquarters.

On her return to Basrah she was assigned to write an outline of recent Arabian history, which she accomplished quickly, glad to have something to do. Her whole being was restless, for here she was, a person accustomed to her own life and to hardships as severe as those of the troops at the front, tied to the routine life of an office stool. She knew that it would be useless to complain and, with a grudge in her heart against red tape, went on conscientiously doing her work and deploring that she was a woman.

Then suddenly her whole outlook changed. On March 10, 1917, Baghdad fell to the Anglo-Indian troops and a few days later she received orders to join Sir Percy Cox. Gertrude was at last to have the opportunity for which she longed and to carve her name into the history of Asia.

CHAPTER XII

ONCE AGAIN THE MINARETS OF BAGHDAD set a flashing welcome over the Tigris, once more the breeze whispering through the palm trees was hushed as the ancient city of Haroun al Raschid awaited the coming of the boat which brought the woman who was now to fulfil her destiny and restore the faded splendour of the Abode of Peace.

Gertrude arrived in Baghdad to find it a mass of roses, in the midst of which harassed officials tried to clear up the mess left behind by the retreating Turks. The inhabitants seemed to be relieved to have the British with them and there were many who gave Gertrude a personal welcome.

Sir Percy Cox came down to meet his collaborator and took her to her home-to-be, which was an empty house in the bazaar. All the British officials were lodged in a haphazard sort of way. This was chiefly owing to the fact that the Baghdadis, no longer having to deal with Oriental administrators who seized anything they wanted, were taking advantage of the Occidentals, who paid for everything and were particular not to offend susceptibilities . . . Gertrude, knowing the ways of the people of the East, at once understood what was happening. She said nothing to Sir Percy, but on the day following her arrival she set about looking after herself, as if she was once more travelling alone.

Visits to a few cafés, several cups of coffee, a little listening to the bazaar talk, led her to a friend of her previous visit called Musa Chalabi. Musa accepted Gertrude's rebuke about the accommodation supplied to the British in smiling silence. He then led her to a garden all golden and pink and scarlet in its mantle of roses and showed her a house. For a moment Gertrude silently looked about her, carried away from prosaic house-hunting to a similar setting in Persia many years before. Then, quickly returning to practical considerations, she examined the place critically, disguising her delight, and said that it might do if the kitchen was renovated and a bathroom built. Musa nodded and replied that that went without saying if she liked the house. An agreement was drawn up and Gertrude set about furnishing her new home. This was no problem either. She knew the bazaar, she knew the merchants and, above all, she understood their bargaining mentality.

Without showing any signs of being in a hurry or even needing anything, she dropped in at the shop of a Baghdadi ostensibly to pay a morning call. Over coffee and a nargileh they chatted about the doings in the town and the future of Mesopotamia. Presently the real object of the visit was broached and set aside as unworthy of a discussion between friends. After a while the shopman laid before his visitor a bundle of embroideries, which were politely examined, with a few complimentary words about their beauty. Then, suddenly, as if the idea had just crossed his mind the merchant produced the things which Gertrude had come to buy, and business started in earnest. A price was suggested to which Gertrude politely made a counter offer and received the answer that at such a figure the goods would be traded at a loss. Gertrude finished her coffee, and thanking the man for showing her such beautiful things, which were much too good for her, left. Their parting was of the most cordial, as if the interlude of doing business had merely been a method of passing the time. But, as Gertrude expected, the merchant returned her call a few days later and, in the course of conversation, mentioned a lower price for the things which Gertrude wanted to buy.

To a British official this method of shopping would seem unnecessarily tedious, but, by following the Oriental custom, Gertrude not only obtained better things cheaper, but became an intimate of the bazaar, the centre of political intrigue and, in half an hour, could find out what it would take an Intelligence officer days to piece together inaccurately.

By the time the bargaining over furniture and draperies had materialized into purchases, the necessary improvements had been made to the house, so Gertrude moved into her home with the kind of servants who would work twice as hard and for half the wages in the service of someone who understood their peculiarities and could talk their language.

From that day on, her garden became the centre of informal intercourse, social and political. Even the holiest men in the district came to call on her, men of widespread influence who were usually not accessible to infidel officials and could, if they wished, do the British cause infinite harm. One of these she described as "so holy that he couldn't look an unveiled woman in the face! It didn't prevent him from desiring to have a long talk with me on private affairs, and at the end, I'll admit he tipped me a casual wink or two, just enough to know me again."

It was this personal contact, this understanding of Oriental problems, which made Gertrude invaluable to her colleagues and relieved the government at home of many responsibilities in connection with the reorganization of the conquered territories. Sir Percy Cox was the ablest of administrators who understood the Arab question as well as Gertrude, but he had always been an official and, however informal he might be with the native, his rank could not be forgotten. The position of Great Britain in the Near East was exceedingly delicate and the least false move or the offending of someone with influence could undo the moral effect of the victories of the army.

Fahad Bey, paramount Sheik of the Amarah, a tribe of tremendous importance, arrived in Baghdad. No one quite knew how he should be treated, until Gertrude remembered that she had stayed with him three years before in the desert, so when he appeared she greeted him as an old friend. The rest was simple. She returned his hospitality, talked to him about the things which interested him, without reference to politics, and eventually took him to Government House. Sir Percy complimented Fahad Bey on the loyalty of his tribesmen to the British cause, but the sheik disclaimed responsibility and bowed towards Gertrude. His Bedouins knew Gertrude and when he had read them a letter which she had written from Basrah, someone had said: "If this is from a woman, what must her men be like!"

Having paid this graceful compliment, he presented Gertrude with two beautiful Arab greyhounds. Later on he was taken to see a demonstration of flying by the R.A.F. which intrigued him to such an extent that he asked if he might get into an airplane, but added that on no account must it be allowed to leave the ground as he was shortly to wed two new wives.

Fahad Bey was at that time nearly eighty!

A few days later two old sheiks, poor and ragged, made their appearance in Baghdad. Their territory was on the borderland of Mesopotamia and they had alternately been harried by the British and the Turks and never knew who were their masters. As soon as the Turks retreated for good, the British, without making any investigations, put all the tribesmen in a prison concentration camp. The two old men were in despair and did not know to whom they could appeal until they heard that Gertrude was in Baghdad. They journeyed there at once and she found them piteously waiting in her rose garden. As soon as she had heard their story she went straight to Sir Percy Cox and the injustices were remedied. The old sheiks wept with gratitude and offered her a thoroughbred mare which she had to refuse, so they sent her a gazelle instead, which ruined the roses and ate up many of the official documents and maps.

This knowledge of the working of the Arab mind enabled her also to deal with cases which an official might have overlooked as unworthy of attention. But she knew how rapidly news travelled over the desert by word of mouth and an unintentional slight to someone who did not seem to matter could be exaggerated and spread all over the country.

An old chief from the Syrian side of the desert came one day knocking at the gates of Government House, demanding to see the High Commissioner. No one had ever heard of this man and he did not look important, in fact he appeared to be a lunatic. News of what was happening reached

Gertrude and, sensing an impending tactless blunder, she went off to investigate. Having calmed the old chap's ravings she inquired the motive of his journey, which he readily told her.

Travelling across the desert he had met a woman of stupendous stature and luminous countenance. On being questioned as to her identity she declared she was the sun, but this reply did not satisfy the old chief and, pressing her further, she admitted that she was the British Government. Thereat he resolved to come straight to Kokus (Sir Percy Cox) seeking the sun.

Gertrude accepted the story in all solemnity and at once arranged an interview with "Kokus," and the old gentleman returned to his tribe a hero and made heroes of the British.

An unexpected outcome of this incident was to cause the name "Kokus" to become an accepted word in the Arabic language as a title. Any man of position and worthy of respect was soon referred to as "a Kokus," while Gertrude had the signal honour of being known as Kokusah!

One day the guide who had led Gertrude from Hayil arrived at her house to pay his respects. Gertrude had never been able to reward him for saving her life from the raiders and bringing her caravan safely through the desert to Baghdad, so she now gave him a heavily embroidered cloak. The temperature was standing at 122, but the nomad was so proud at receiving this gift that he spent the day parading the town wrapped in the stifling garment.

Another day one of the Damascenes who had accompanied Gertrude throughout the whole of the Hayil expedition turned up and, without discussion, took his place in her household as if they had never been parted. These people of Arabia and Asia Minor regarded Gertrude as a sort of elder sister, who understood their problems, scolded or comforted and, while meeting them on an equal footing, never let them forget that she was the eldest. This familiar contact with all classes enabled her to feel the pulse of Iraq and diagnose symptoms much quicker than her more highly placed colleagues and at the same time gave her devoted friends among the Baghdadis. The most intimate of these was an old man called Haji Naji who, to the officials, was just a gardener who raised fruits and vegetables on the banks of the Tigris, but to Gertrude represented the mind of Baghdad. Their friendship began with a present of a pruning knife, which Sir Hugh Bell had sent out from England, and, from then on, his garden became a refuge for Gertrude whenever she was tired of State building. Sometimes she would relax and watch the old man at his work, on other occasions she would gossip about what was being said and thought in Baghdad. Frequently she would take British officials to the garden by the Tigris to show them that the humbler Baghdadis were not all ignorant coolies and also to let Haji Naji realize that the British administrators were more than automatons in uniform.

In order to help make matters pertaining to their future even clearer to the populations newly under British rule, Gertrude was instrumental in starting a newspaper in Arabic for which she wrote the leading articles. Everyone in Baghdad wanted to help and she could have had the equivalent in numbers of the staff of a London daily paper without anyone expecting a salary! The editor was H. St. J. Philby, an Indian Civil Servant on Sir Percy's staff and one of the greatest authorities on Arabia, who knew the country as well as Gertrude and was consequently an ideal collaborator.[1]

All this work had to be carried out in a climate which is merciless to Occidentals and with fever which lays the victim down in an hour and leaves him weak for days. The heat made recuperation slow and there was too much to do to allow any reasonable period for convalescence. Gertrude found herself at the end of the summer worn out and her hair beginning to turn grey. Luckily she had had the forethought to have herself inoculated against cholera and plague which, every now and then, treacherously struck at the cities of Mesopotamia. She had seen cholera and all its attendant horrors at close quarters in Persia and when, one night just before a dinner at Government House, the Commander-in-Chief, Sir Stanley Maude, was taken violently ill she knew what to expect. Forty-eight hours later the conqueror of Baghdad, perhaps one of the greatest generals which the war produced, had died in the same room where von der Goltz, the German Commander-in-Chief, had passed away two years earlier.

It was in these times of ill-health that Gertrude knew the loneliness of being without woman companionship. While well and working, the men sufficed, but there were occasions when they got on her nerves. The only two friends she had of her own sex were the matron of the military hospital and the Mother Superior of the Dominican Convent, a French woman from Touraine.

She made a few attempts to get the women of Baghdad together, but although the foreigners co-operated and the

[1] Since those days Mr. Philby has retired from public life and, having become a Moslem, spends most of his time in the desert living with the Arabs.

Moslems showed polite enthusiasm and did their best to chat with the Europeans, the Eastern and Western conceptions of life were too far apart to make the experiment a success. Besides, the nuns and the nurses had more work than they could cope with and only relaxed when they slept.

When the matron herself succumbed to the terrible climate and after a short illness died, Gertrude felt desolate, but refused to give in or take a rest at home.

> "They gave her a military funeral," she wrote, "with the bugle call of the Last Post and the salute of rifles into empty air. And I hoped as I walked behind the Union Jack that covered her coffin that when people walked behind my coffin it would be with thoughts dimly resembling those I gave to her . . ."

She never seemed to realize her own position or appreciate what she was doing for her country. When she was made a Companion of the Order of the British Empire, was authorized to wear the war medals and was four times "mentioned in despatches," she replied to the congratulations that these rewards were "singularly preposterous"!

The year 1917 came to an end with disappointment that peace had not been signed. America was pouring troops into France, but their weight had not been felt and the Central Powers still held out. In the Orient the war was to all intents and purposes over, but the programme of administration of the conquered territories was being held up owing to the uncertainty as to the outcome of hostilities on the Western Front. All that Gertrude could do was to continue drawing up her reports on the tribes and keeping in touch with those chiefs who would be helpful when the time came to form the proposed Arab Government.

She discovered Colonel Leachman who, like Gertrude,

was an expert on all Arab questions. Leachman had been a subaltern in the Sussex Regiment in India before the war, where his gift for Oriental languages and an amazing ability to disguise himself as a Frontier tribesman caused him to be seconded for service with the Intelligence Corps. He had no fear and would penetrate the border among Afghans and Afridis where no white man had ever been. Leachman appealed to Gertrude in the same way as Lawrence, and together they perfected the plans for the future administration of Mesopotamia.

Gertrude's talks with Leachman made her realize that if Mesopotamia was to become an independent state under British protection the youth of the country must learn that Islam was not the most important thing in the world. So she encouraged the formation of schools in which the Koran was not the only textbook and tried to make the Arabs send their children to be educated. The experiment was not entirely successful. The attendance was fair but the ability to absorb what was being taught or to see things from a non-Islamic point of view was disappointing. Gertrude used to visit the school to see how the pupils were getting on and occasionally test their general knowledge. The first question she asked was who was King of England. After an awkward silence one of the small pupils suggested Chosroes, one of the founders of the early Persian dynasties, while another with a better grasp of modern politics said that it was Lloyd George!

She was more successful in getting the people to look after their health. The news that hospitals and dispensaries were being opened in Baghdad, where the Arabs could receive medicine and free treatment, spread rapidly throughout the length and breadth of the desert and in a very short time the doctors could not cope with the mobs which came for medical advice.

In the midst of all this anxious work of reorganization Gertrude made time to keep up her archaeology and examined ruins and copied inscriptions whenever she had the opportunity. She took Lord and Lady Willingdon, the future Viceroy and Vicereine of India, to Babylon and told how the city had been built about 2000 B.C. by Nimrod and one thousand years later, under Nebuchadnezzar, had spread out on either side of the Euphrates until it covered a larger area than Greater London. It was here that the lovely Semiramis had the famous hanging gardens constructed, which were classified as one of the seven wonders of the world. She showed them how the excavators and geologists had been able to establish the various eras in Babylon's history beginning with the period of the Deluge, the traces of which were still clearly visible. Her talk was so entertaining that a member of the viceregal staff, who had set out on the expedition saying he hated ruins, admitted, after the lecture, that there must be something in archaeology after all.

Gertrude could not be spared to take a holiday in England, but a change of air was imperative, so she decided to leave Baghdad for part of the summer.

She had longed to go back to Persia and revisit Gulahek. Twenty-six years had passed since she had left in high hopes of returning as the wife of Henry Cadogan, twenty-six years of doing the things which they had planned to do together. She felt that perhaps the revisiting of old scenes would give her more strength for the struggle ahead.

The journey did her endless good. She travelled to Kirmashah and on to Gulahek and Tehran. She walked the old walks, rode again to the lovely gardens and fished the streams where she had fished with Henry. The memories were poignantly beautiful and brought renewed vigour to the tired middle-aged woman.

But if it was not possible for her to go to England she did not forget her family and always found time to write long letters about what she was doing. Heat or cold or illness never impaired her style or lost her that aptitude for vivid description.

"We have had a week of fierce heat, temperature 122 odd and therewith a burning wind which has to be felt to be believed. It usually blows all night as well as all day and makes sleep very difficult. I have invented a scheme which I practise on the worst nights. I drop a sheet in water and without wringing it out lay it in a pile along my bed between me and the wind. I put one end over my feet and draw the other under and over my head and leave the rest a few inches from my body. The sharp evaporation makes it icy cold and interposes a little wall of cold air between me and the fierce wind. When it dries I wake up and repeat the process.

"I don't know whether it is a scientific truth but it's undoubtedly in accordance with facts—full moon nights are by far the hottest and stillest. Two nights ago I was completely defeated. I tried to work sitting outside in my garden after dinner, but after half an hour the few clothes I was wearing were wringing wet and I was so much exhausted by a day similarly spent that I went to bed helplessly and fell asleep at once on my roof. I hadn't been asleep long when I woke up to find the Great Bear staring me in the face. It was very strange to see the Great Bear shining so brilliantly in the full moon of Ramadhan and while I wondered half asleep what had happened I realized that the whole of the world was dark, and turning round saw the last limb of the moon disappearing in a total eclipse. So I lay watching it, a wonderful sight, the disc just visible, a dull and angry copper colour. In the bazaar a few hundred yards away everyone was drumming with sticks on anything that lay handy, to scare away the devil which hid the moon, and indeed they ultimately succeeded, for after a long, long time the upper limb of the moon reappeared and the devil drew slowly downwards, angry still with deep red tongues, and wreaths projecting from his copper coloured body and before I had time to sleep again the Ramadhan moon had once more extinguished the shining Bear . . ."

In the autumn of 1918 she received a great disappointment. It was announced that Sir Percy Cox, who had gone to England to confer with the Government, was not returning to Baghdad. He had been appointed to Tehran. The information staggered Gertrude, causing her momentarily to feel discouraged and lose interest in her work. Sir Percy had become a kind of God to her. They had been colleagues for a long time and had gone through many trials together. They were in complete sympathy, each had the other's confidence, and their relationship was much more than that of chief and subordinate.

She had hardly had time to get over the shock of losing Sir Percy when the armistice was signed. The event which brought the greatest war in history to a close passed almost unnoticed in Baghdad as fighting, from an active point of view, had long ceased in Mesopotamia. What did set the whole place in a ferment was the Franco-British declaration. Many promises had been made during the time that the co-operation of the sheiks was wanted in the waging of war against the Turks, but the majority of the well-informed Mesopotamians had regarded these as so much bait. So when it was proclaimed that the future of the Arab states was in the inhabitants' hands and they could choose the form of government they preferred, no one knew what to say.

At first the people divided themselves into two factions, those who believed that the country would best be ruled by Sir Percy Cox with Gertrude Bell as his assistant, and those who regarded an Arab Emir as the only possible head of the Government. There were also a few groups with republican tendencies and some who regretted the Turks, but the two main factions were those which, for the moment, counted.

To Gertrude fell the task of unravelling the somewhat nebulous and impractical desires of the tribal chiefs and the citizens of the towns, and, as she at once predicted, these questions took a very long time to settle. In the meanwhile, she was called to Paris to attend the Peace Conference and left Baghdad at the beginning of 1919. She had been in the Orient for over four consecutive years without a break.

Before boarding the ship which was to carry her to Europe she tried to find traces of Fattuh, who had been caught up in the war on the side of the enemy. There was little definite information to be had, but it seemed clear that the faithful cook and companion had been killed. Gertrude was very upset at hearing this news, but she had no time to make any further inquiries as the allied peace delegates were gathering in Paris, ready to carve up the world according to their appetites, and Gertrude wanted to be there and ensure that her little section was not hacked about by inexperienced knife wielders.

PART IV

THE BIRTH OF IRAQ

CHAPTER XIII

The Congress of Vienna is said to have danced. It cannot be predicted how historians will refer to the Paris Peace Conference, but it did not take life very seriously. "The Paris Peace Conference made whoopee" might be the most appropriate term for the chief occupation of its delegates.

Gertrude had spent four years in desert surroundings and a wartime atmosphere, with few of those comforts to which a woman is accustomed. Lawrence had achieved the impossible with his Arab irregulars and had become a legendary figure. Doctor Hogarth's dreams had materialized without the public being aware of his existence. The Emir Faisal was on his way to a throne, of which Lawrence had laid the foundations and which Gertrude was to make into a permanent edifice.

These four people met in the over-decorated rooms of the British Delegation's headquarters at the Hotel Majestic in Paris and gazed wonderingly at the Peace Makers! Lawrence, looking more emaciated than ever in his Arab headdress, scornful of all this pleasure-seeking after the grim days of war on the desert; Faisal, tall and aristocratic in his robes, thoroughly entertained by the spectacle of Occidentals enjoying themselves, and longing to join them; Hogarth, bearded and rugged, wanting only to be out of uniform and back in the peaceful atmosphere of Oxford; Gertrude in her smart, new dresses, interested in everything about her. Lawrence and his scorn, Faisal and his enthusiasm, Hogarth and his stolid learning, the old delegates trying to be young, the young delegates trying to seem important, the chic of the women, the tedious conferences, the parties and the shops of Paris coming to life after four years of mourning—everything which Gertrude saw and did, as usual, enthralled her.

It was a curious quartet, all with the same interests at heart, but thinking of them from different points of view. Hogarth archaeologically and historically; Faisal nationalistically and ambitiously; Lawrence idealistically and impractically; Gertrude practically and constructively.

The fact that Lawrence disappeared from the Arabian picture and Gertrude lived to see the dreams of an independent kingdom realized was because they approached the problem from different angles. Both of them had Arabia in their blood, but whereas Lawrence had never known any other ideals in his life, Gertrude was a woman of the world who had judgement and poise. Lawrence became a crank about the Arabs; he became bitter when those in power disregarded his projects, and retired into a futile state of wasting his life in a lost cause and died ignominiously on a motor bicycle.

Gertrude realized that no one in Europe really cared what happened to the Arabs who had helped the Allies win the war, but moping about it would not help. The word of Britain had been given to the Arabs and, even if the European problems which confronted the delegates at the time appeared to be of paramount importance, this word would be kept, if for no other reason than that the desert people were still a vital cog in the British Empire's complicated machinery.

Gertrude and Lawrence were actually both idealists, but Lawrence's attitude was that of a man who can only see his love as something of the immediate passionate present, while Gertrude more logically and femininely regarded Arabia as a mate who could be with her always.

She acted accordingly.

Having ascertained the attitude of the British and explained to them in detail exactly what the problems were, and would be, in Mesopotamia, she called on the French Government.

The French interests in Syria were contiguous to the British and, although the former had quite different ideas as to how they would administer their mandate, the two countries would have to stand together, at least outwardly. This contact with the French was an astute move as it gave Gertrude an excellent insight into certain delicate problems which she would have to face when she got back to Mesopotamia.

Before returning to the Orient, Gertrude allowed herself to relax and had her last real rest. She motored all through the battle fields of Northern France and Belgium with her father and then went into quiet seclusion in Yorkshire for the rest of the summer. At the beginning of the autumn she started back to her Arabs.

She did not travel direct, but stopped at Cairo, and at Jerusalem where she wanted to have a talk with Sir Ronald Storrs, whom she had known when he was Oriental Secretary of the Residency in Cairo. She found everyone too deeply immersed in the new problems of Zionism to pay any attention to the future of Mesopotamia, so she made for Damascus and then to Aleppo. In Aleppo she received joyous news!

Fattuh was alive after all! He looked old and haggard and had evidently had a hard time. When Gertrude had parted from him after the journey to Hayil he was comparatively well to do, but he now had only a horse and a small cart in which he transported wood to sell in Aleppo. At first he would not talk of the bad times on which he had fallen, but after a while he confessed that because of his years of service with Gertrude the Turks had taken all he possessed. Gertrude did all she could for her old servant and dined with him and his wife in their tiny house. Proudly Fattuh produced some of the cups and camp kit which had belonged to the Hayil caravan and far into the night the Englishwoman and the Arab cook reminisced about the good old days. As they parted, Fattuh said:

"O Lady, our hearts were so light when we travelled; now they are so heavy a camel could not carry us."

Gertrude reached Baghdad at the beginning of November 1919 and took up her work exactly where she had left off. She had undertaken the task of seeing the country through its period of labour and had banished all idea of going home until this was over. Realizing that this would take a long time, she had ordered crockery and furniture when in England to make her Baghdad house more comfortable.

The situation was very confused owing to the uncertainty of the eventual status of Iraq, the now official name for Mesopotamia. From Gertrude's point of view it was rendered all the more difficult owing to the fact that she did not see eye to eye with the new High Commissioner, Sir Arnold Wilson.

Before the Paris Peace Conference, Sir Percy Cox had taken up his post in Tehran and Gertrude felt that she had been deprived of the collaboration of the one man who could carry out the reorganization of Iraq. She had formed an opinion, as soon as she met Wilson, that he was the wrong man for the difficult work to be done; and consequently she resented his presence at Government House. When she returned to the East these feelings about Sir Arnold increased until they verged on those of insubordination. She allowed no one in Baghdad to suspect that there were any differences of opinion between herself and her chief, but this did not prevent her writing about the situation to her superiors in England. The fact that this extremely unorthodox procedure did not cause her to be recalled shows how highly she must have been esteemed. That Gertrude was right in her views was shown by the displacement of Wilson at the end of 1920 and the return of Cox to the office of High Commissioner.

It has been suggested that Gertrude was an intriguer who made use of her connections in high places in England. This is not true, for though she did report confidentially and direct to the seat of authority, when she considered the circumstances warranted it, it was not to further her own ends but because she knew she was right. In the same way, the recipients of Gertrude's letters took heed of what she said because it had been proved that, in matters connected with the Arabs, she was rarely wrong.

The biggest problem which confronted the British administrators who were trying to form some sort of government was the attitude of the various religious elements in the country, notably that of the fanatical Shiah sect.

The Mohammedan religion which began, like all other Faiths of the world, united in its beliefs, soon found itself divided into dissenting factions. While these dissensions did not divide Islam to the same extent as the various sects of Christianity, the three main groups became and remained essentially individual.

The largest of the three groups is the Sunnis, who hold that the Caliphate of Islam (the head of the religion) is an elective office and must be held by a member of the Koreish tribe to which the Prophet belonged.

The Sunnis have various other doctrines peculiar to their sect, but their main basis of differing with the next most important group of Moslems, the Shiahs, is in this question of the Caliphate.

The Shiahs maintain that the head of the Faith is a God-given office and belongs to the descendants of Ali, Mohammed's adopted son who married his favourite daughter Fatima. The antagonistic attitude of the Shiahs towards the other Islamic sects is further enhanced by the fact that a great many of the adherents are converted Persians who brought with them many of their political as well as religious doctrines. (Most of the Shiahs in Baghdad were Persian subjects which added complications to the complicated situation, but also enabled their non-inclusion in the government on the grounds that they were not Mesopotamian citizens.)

The third main Mohammedan sect is known as the

Khawarij, but its followers, living chiefly in Eastern Arabia and North Africa, had nothing to do with the situation in Baghdad.

The greater part of Gertrude's life in the Orient had been spent among the Mohammedans of the desert who were practically all Sunnis, and she leaned instinctively towards them. These friendly feelings were further increased by the recollections of the Shiah mentality which she had encountered in Hayil. The situation was made even more complex by the fact that, whereas among Mohammedans of the world as a whole the Sunnis formed by far the greatest proportion, in Iraq it was the Shiahs who predominated.

Gertrude herself was handicapped as the fact of her being unveiled precluded any practical contact with the dignitaries of the Shiahs. Neither could she have any intimate relations with the women who regarded her as a kind of man, and always veiled themselves in her presence and refused to talk. It was an impossible predicament; she was too female for the men and too male for the women!

She knew, however, that until these fiercely pan-Islamic and anti-British people were won over there would always be trouble. She accordingly decided to undermine this fortress of bigotry.

There was in Baghdad a Shiah whom Gertrude suspected of inclinations towards free thought. She had met him several times and done him one or two small services. Gradually she flattered and cajoled the man until she was able to persuade him to ask Saiyid Hassan, the head of the most important Shiah family in the district, to see her.

Hassan was much taken aback by the request; but, his curiosity having been aroused, he agreed to receive Gertrude in his home. Her feelings as she crossed the threshold of this fanatic's house were similar to those she had experienced when the Kaiser received her in his box at the theatre in Berlin, but she did not falter and went straight on to the reception room. She found Saiyid Hassan as formidable a figure as William II, with a white beard reaching down to the middle of his chest and the biggest turban she had ever seen. After the formal salutations Hassan bade Gertrude sit down on the carpet beside him, and they began to talk generalities: first of all, intimately about his health and guardedly about his family, then about Arab and Persian literature and the collections of Oriental books in London and Paris and Rome. The man was not only extremely well educated but a brilliant conversationalist.

After nearly an hour of talking Gertrude thought that this was long enough for a first visit so she prepared to leave, but the old man protested that he had set aside the whole afternoon for her. So Gertrude resumed her place on the carpet, and, emboldened by the friendly attitude, began to tell her host of the project to make Iraq into a kingdom with Faisal as its first king. Hassan listened attentively, but objected when he heard that the French would remain in Beyrouth. Gertrude changed the conversation diplomatically and they discussed the evils of Bolshevism!

When she eventually said goodbye, Hassan rose and said majestically:

"It is well-known that you are the most learned woman of your time, and if any proof were needed it would be found in the fact that you wish to frequent the society of the learned. That is why you are here today. You may come and see me as often as you like."

Gertrude thanked her host and left. As she walked through the dim, narrow streets of the quarter where these fanatics lived she felt greatly relieved, for she knew that the British Government would have less trouble with the Shiahs.

A few weeks later her longed-for wish to have her father to herself and in her own surroundings was fulfilled, when he came out to Iraq to pay his daughter a visit. He was made a great deal of by all her Arab friends, being treated not as Sir Hugh Bell of Rounton Grange in the county of Yorkshire, but as the honoured father of Gertrude Bell of the Arabian desert!

Shortly after Sir Hugh's departure, Fattuh arrived in Baghdad and took over Gertrude's kitchen and the organization of her household as he had the desert caravans. Turning to Gertrude as they chatted about old times, he inquired:

"Is his excellency the progenitor still in Baghdad?"

And on Gertrude asking how he knew that her father had been in Iraq, she learned that he had heard it from a Bedouin he had encountered miles away in the desert! Everything pertaining to Gertrude was of interest to the Arabs.

However, in spite of her having penetrated into the Shiah camp, matters were far from settled. The Nationalists were on the warpath, advocating independence without a mandate. Meetings were being held daily in the mosques, with agitators making impassioned speeches on the unity of Islam and the rights of the Arab race. The atmosphere became so tense that not even Gertrude ventured into the bazaar. The situation was not made any easier by the attitude of the people at home. A large section of the British press was advocating giving in to the demands of the patriots in Iraq and evacuating the country regardless of the losses.

Sir Percy Cox accordingly decided to go to England and, before leaving, he sent for Gertrude and explained to her that he intended to fight to the last on a no-surrender policy. Quite apart from the huge monetary losses which any abandonment of the mandate would entail, it would also mean the return of the Turks, with the Arabs falling once more under their unscrupulous domination. Sir Percy did not disguise his qualms about the successful issue of his mission and warned Gertrude that it might become physically dangerous for her to remain in Baghdad. At the same time he made it clear that he would not feel easy in his mind if she were not in Iraq. Gertrude naturally remained, scoffing at any possibility of harm coming to her. There was no element of fear in Gertrude's character and she could make light of the most precarious situations. At the end of a letter describing the momentous things which were happening, she wrote:

"I am going to keep Lady Cox's parrot while she is away. I should feel easier in my mind if I were quite sure that my cook would not look on it as a species of chicken and eat it . . ."

And while on this subject of birds and the Coxes, she writes:

"I must tell you another nice tale about the Coxes. You know he is a great naturalist. He is making a collection of all Mesopotamian birds—sometimes they arrive dead and sometimes alive. The last one was alive. It's a huge eagle, not yet in its grown plumage, but for all that the largest fowl I've ever set eyes on. It lives on a perch on the shady side of the house and it eats bats, mainly. These bats are netted for it in the dusk when they obligingly fly across the river and over Sir Percy's garden wall. But the eagle likes to eat them in the morning, so the long-suffering Lady Cox keeps them in a tin in her ice chest, and if ever you've heard before of an eagle that lives on iced bat you'll please inform me!"

Sir Percy Cox's departure was construed by the Arabs as a sign of weakness and Gertrude found that she would have to deal with a state of mind where the smallest error in judgement might cause a disaster. The propaganda of the Nationalists was making headway with the tribesmen and it was evident that these would soon get out of hand if something drastic were not done. The Baghdadis themselves were in a highly nervous state and prominent citizens were continually calling on Gertrude, urging that firm action be taken as the Nationalists were losing control of the situation. Once the bazaar mob got out of hand, anything might happen.

Gertrude hesitated for a little while and then acted in her quick, determined way. She made it evident to the Government of India that more troops were needed at once if a calamity was to be avoided. This she followed with a local demonstration.

The young Nationalists were staging a patriotic play filled with independence propaganda. Gertrude called together three of the British political officers, told them that she was going to attend the performance and invited them to join her. For a moment the officers demurred and Gertrude quickly added that, whether they decided to come or not, she was going. The officers laughed and followed her into the town.

Gertrude walked into the theatre and took her place

with as much unconcern as if she had been going to a play in Yorkshire. She listened to the attacks on England which were vociferously applauded. When the play was over she went to the actors and congratulated them on the excellence of the performance. For a moment there was a surprised silence, then those Nationalists who were among her friends crowded around her, welcoming her and thanking her for coming. Gertrude had won again, but there had been a few minutes when she had been in great danger, as she learned next evening from an eminent Sunni with Nationalistic tendencies who visited her. As he was leaving he whispered:

"When in Allah's name are you going to release us from the terror of the tribes?"

"Soon," replied Gertrude.

A few days later large reinforcements were moving up the river.

The critical situation had been eased, but it was not over.

Colonel Leachman was ambushed and murdered at the beginning of August and an ominous silence fell over Baghdad as the people waited to see what would be done in reprisal. Gertrude was not too certain as to the wisdom of taking the initiative in a case which might be simple banditry, so she remained inactive but alert. Then, in the middle of August she heard that the extremists were going to stage a monster meeting in Baghdad to be followed by a procession which would undoubtedly lead to disturbances. It was a vital moment when the right action was essential. Force might precipitate a revolt, indifference might give the agitators an idea that they could do as they pleased. Gertrude was called into conference. Without hesitation, she advocated force. The result of this advice was the arrest of the ringleaders, the forbidding of all meetings and a curfew over Baghdad. In twenty-four hours Baghdad had returned to its lazy, Oriental, fatalistic self.

Humphrey Bowman, the director of education in Iraq, gives a description of Gertrude's calm demeanour at this time when every white man felt that he was sitting on a bomb about to explode.

In an attempt to make the various political rivals feel that the British wanted to settle the fortunes of the country impartially, Sir Edgar Bonham-Carter, the acting High Commissioner, gave an "at home."

A large number of Arab notables, many of whom were hostile to England, sat round the room, awkwardly making conversation with a sprinkling of Englishmen who were evidently ill at ease. The talk had almost completely flagged when the door opened and Gertrude came in, beautifully dressed, and looking as if she had just left Park Lane. Everyone rose and she walked round the room, shaking hands with each Arab in turn and saying a few appropriate words to each. Not only did she know them all by name—there must have been forty in the room—but all about their families and occupations. The tension eased, and when the party broke up the farewells were as cordial as the greetings had been frigid.

Fahad Bey, who had given Gertrude the greyhounds, also went out of his way to write to her, saying that nothing could compel him to alter his allegiance to her and to England.

Still there was nothing to warrant any real optimism, and throughout that torrid summer of 1920 Gertrude worked on regardless of physical discomforts. The Shiahs were keeping their promise to support her or, at any rate, remain neutral, but their authority was weakening. The principles of the Jihad—the holy war—were being implanted by fanatics into the minds of the tribesmen, and the unthinking populace was blindly following unscrupulous leaders to revolt. The few revolutionaries who listened to Gertrude's pleas for moderation to give the High Commissioner time to return to Iraq and tell them of the results of his mission to London, argued that Europe's latest methods of demonstrating the advantage of modern civilization were hardly convincing, especially to a nation much older than any of the West.

Even Gertrude, who usually had a retort for arguments of this nature, felt baffled.

> "We've practically come to the collapse of society here," she wrote, "and there's little on which you can depend for its reconstruction. The credit of European civilization is gone. Over and over again people have said that it has been a shock and a surprise to see Europe relapse into barbarism. I had no reply—what else can you call war? How can we, who have managed our affairs so badly, claim to teach others to manage theirs better? It may be that the world has need to sink back into the dark ages of chaos out of which we will evolve something, perhaps no better than what it had!"

The criticism of the more reasonable Arabs was that Great Britain had promised self-governing institutions and not only had taken no steps towards creating them but was busily setting up something quite different. One of the local papers came out openly with a leading article, stating that England had promised an Arab Government with British advisers and had set up a British Government with so-called Arab advisers.

Gertrude could find nothing plausible with which to refute this, so she said nothing and, keeping her head, continued to bluff until Sir Percy Cox returned from England.

CHAPTER XIV

Sir Percy Cox arrived in Iraq from London on October 12, 1920, and was splendidly received at the railway station by the majority of the Baghdad notables and a number of desert sheiks.

As soon as the ceremonies of welcome were over, Sir Percy had a private conference with Gertrude and, thanking her for all she had done during his absence, spoke optimistically of his visit to England. He had come back with full authority to set up an Arab government with British advisers to the native ministers. The first big question now was, whom to appoint as Premier. Gertrude suggested that the notables be consulted without delay, pointing out the imperative urgency of getting something constructive done. Sir Percy promised to waste no time and Gertrude went home to sleep soundly for the first time for months, knowing that a man was now at the helm in whose judgement she and all the normal-thinking Arabs had complete confidence.

The next day, however, there were complications again. The reception at the railway station had been bungled. The most important chiefs, who had had access to the platform, had shaken hands with Sir Percy, but all the less important had been herded together in a dusty enclosure outside the station and had only caught a glimpse of the High Commissioner as he entered his car.

"We came in love and obedience," exclaimed an old sheik, "and when we tried to get near his Excellency we were pushed away."

When Gertrude heard of this she went cold all through, in spite of the heat. This kind of small slight was most difficult to remedy and would spread over the desert more rapidly than an incident with a high-ranking Arab official who knew something of the ways of the West. She went at once to report what had happened to Mr. Philby; he took up the matter with Sir Percy, who at once asked Gertrude to do anything she thought fit to put things right.

In going into the grievances of the sheiks, Gertrude discovered that there was an enormous number of other people who should have had personal contact with the High Commissioner, and any discrimination would only aggravate the ill-feeling. So she arranged interviews to take place in relays of thirties, and while Sir Percy was receiving one group, Gertrude was entertaining the next to coffee and conversation in the adjoining room. The whole idea worked out successfully and the ill-feeling was dispelled. The goodwill of the Baghdadis was further enhanced by the news that British troops had won a victory over the dissident tribes which were now ready to make submission.

The question as to who should be first prime minister now came up again. The Naquib—or, to quote his full title, His Reverence Saiyid Abdurrahman Effendi, the Naquib (chief noble) of Baghdad—one of the most important religious notables in Iraq and head of the Sunni community, seemed to be the most obvious person.

He traced his descent from Hussain, the grandson of the Prophet, who had for a while been Khalif of Iraq.

The Naquib was an old friend of Gertrude and had conferred on her the rather tiresome honour of looking after his nargileh—which was continually breaking and flooding his rooms and wasting so much of her time that she had to create a department in the municipality to take over these holy, though messy, duties.

Gertrude agreed with the choice for prime minister, although she remarked confidentially that Sir Percy would be held responsible no matter who was placed at the head of the government. It seemed doubtful, however, whether the Naquib would involve himself in these experiments in state building. The great thing was to have something settled quickly while the people were in the right mood.

Unfortunately Gertrude was taken ill with bronchitis at this critical juncture and Sir Percy's many administrative duties caused negotiations with embryo prime ministers to come to a standstill. The notables were in despair until the Mayor of Baghdad decided that he must see Gertrude, sick or well. She received him in her dressing gown and heard the bazaar gossip. In spite of feeling desperately ill she knew the significance of this chatter and realized that if she gave in now the work of years might crumble and fall. So she told the Mayor to send all those who wished to talk to her to her house.

Thus lying on her sofa she gave audiences. Fahad Bey, who was one of her first visitors, had a simple and futile plan to settle all the difficulties. He was followed by Ali Sulaiman (the head Sheik of the Dulaim, one of the great figures in Iraq and a staunch friend of England) with a better solution than Fahad's, but one far from practical. A host of sheiks from the Tigris and Euphrates valleys swarmed into the sickroom and, after all talking at once, went away with the impression that they would have a government of Iraq according to their lights. In the evening Sir Percy Cox and his staff came to hear what Gertrude had discovered, and not until late at night was she allowed to rest.

Gertrude's last visitor before matters were finally settled was a man of great importance. It was Jaafar Pasha whose background of adventure was even more amazing than Lawrence's.

A Baghdadi born, he had joined the Turko-German armies at the outbreak of war and had proved himself so brilliant a leader that when Enver Pasha wanted someone to organize the Senussi levies he had been chosen. Shipped to Africa in a submarine he led the desert tribesmen in successful actions against the British until he was captured by the Dorsetshire Yeomanry and imprisoned in Cairo. He at once made an attempt to escape but fell, getting out of the window, and broke his ankle which led to his recapture. While convalescing in the hospital he read in the papers of Lawrence's and Faisal's revolt in the desert and of the Turks' reprisals against Arab Nationalists. A sudden doubt came over him that he might be fighting on the wrong side, and as soon as he was able to get about he volunteered to join the British. Sent to Lawrence's headquarters, his personality and prestige made themselves at once felt and imbued the Revolt with new life. Throughout the merciless campaign in Arabia, Jaafar led Faisal's northern army with such brilliance that he was awarded the C.M.G. which was presented to him by General Allenby in person, while his guard of honour was furnished by the Dorsetshire Yeomanry!

Jaafar's support of the new régime in Baghdad was, therefore, of the utmost importance, and Gertrude used all her eloquence to make him see that it was his duty as a patriot to assist in establishing Arab institutions of whatever form his experience told him would be best. If he and others like him acted boldly, relying on British support, the people would follow. Jaafar took his leave, promising his full collaboration.

Jaafar had hardly gone when Sir Percy came joyfully to Gertrude to announce that the Naquib had agreed to form a government. For half an hour Sir Percy and Gertrude sat congratulating each other on the surmounting of their first great obstacle. This relief from anxiety gave Gertrude a good night's rest and set her on the road to recovery.

But although the big obstacle had been surmounted, the tribulations of government making were far from over. The week following the acceptance of the premiership by the Naquib was filled with anxiety, owing to the attitude of various men who thought it was their right to be cabinet ministers. It was rather like dealing with a crowd of children who will not act in a play unless they all have the leading rôles. Jaafar Pasha kept his word and became Minister of Defence, but the members of the different political and religious factions showed obstinacy in giving their disinterested support.

Gertrude was the only person who had the least influence with the creators of controversy. Sir Percy Cox's other political officers would put forward the most convincing arguments and the men concerned would smile enigmatically and not alter their opinions. Then Gertrude would be called in and, casting aside all Oriental etiquette, speak as she had to the Chief Eunuch in Hayil when he would not let her leave the city. The polite smile would disappear and be replaced by an attentive silence as this woman poured out the convictions of her heart. It was the genuineness of this conviction which always won the day. Gertrude loved the Arab people and she wanted to see the country united under their rule, which could only be done by everyone co-operating.

To those who have not lived among Orientals, the tremendous feat which she performed in bringing all the factions together is hard to appreciate. It was not just a matter of new politics, but an upheaval of the customs, which had not changed for centuries, and the unbridling of a people who had always been ruled with a heavy rein. There were the Shiah obscurantists steeped in fanatical prejudices, the genuine enthusiasts like Jaafar Pasha, the young hot-heads who believed in revolution, the polished statesmen who could not see eye to eye with the reformers and the fanatics, the scholars who based all their ideas on tradition, and those who had lived under the tyrannical rule of the Turks and could not clearly visualize an independent government.

Eventually a Cabinet was formed under the Naquib and had its first meeting on November 7, 1920. Everyone was rather ill at ease, without the slightest conception of procedure, and all that was discussed was the relations to be between the ministers and their British advisers.

Sir Percy cleared up this question to the satisfaction of the Cabinet and the ministers settled down to try to carry out a little constructive work. There was immediate trouble from the Shiahs who, owing to their obstinacy, had no member of their sect with a portfolio. A shuffle round had to be made to remedy this. Trouble from the pro-Turkish party, who were ex-Turkish employees and were opposed to any form of Arab government. Trouble from ministers who went behind the Cabinet's back to Sir Percy and Gertrude. The tact and calm of these two were superior to anything Oriental.

Then when the situation seemed to be settling itself, an unexpected bomb fell in the form of tribal risings. Sir Percy's patience deserted him and he ordered immediate military action. These desert people, worked up by fanatics, would not understand anything but force, and as long as they were in the possession of arms they would fight. Some of the staff protested that it would be difficult to explain British troops burning Arab villages at one end of the country and at the other end assuring the people that Great Britain had handed over the rule of Iraq to native ministers. But Sir Percy was adamant in his determination to have peace and replied to his objectors that there would be amnesty, but after submission. His firm stand was rewarded, and after a few round-ups of dissidents the desert, for the moment, relapsed into its proverbial peace.

This particular situation brought up another question, that of a native army which could gradually take over the responsibilities of the British. The difficulty was in getting men to join. The terms of the mandate forbade conscription and it was evident that no one would become a soldier unless he earned as much or more than a civilian of the same status. The matter was placed in the hands of Jaafar Pasha who confidently took over the difficult task and, in less than a year, was able to form an efficient brigade of Iraqui troops.

The next step in the remodelling of the constitution of this ancient country was to establish some sort of electoral law. The problem was handed to Gertrude to work out. The paramount difficulty which at once came up was the representation of the desert and the towns. If the Bedouins were allowed the quota of representatives to which their numbers entitled them, they would swamp the townspeople and the desert would rule. The desert held the majority of the population of Iraq, but a country under the leadership of rival sheiks, with little idea about laws other than those of necessity created in the camp, would soon became chaotic. Gertrude was at first puzzled as to how to get out of the quandary, but, after many conferences with those concerned, an admirable scheme was evolved whereby the representation would be by divisions of the country and not by specified tribes.

This plan was duly put into effect to the general satisfaction of everyone.

Whom to appoint as the ruler of Iraq was the next conundrum to be solved. On Christmas Day 1920 a deputation of the towns' notables and desert chiefs called on Gertrude and asked whom she suggested for their king. Without hesitation, she replied:

"A son of the Sharif, and for choice the Emir Faisal."

The Sharif, to whom Gertrude referred, was Husain Ibn Ali, the Emir of Mecca and the chief instrument in bringing about Lawrence's Revolt in the Desert. At this time he was King of the Hejaz, but liked to style himself King of the Arab countries. Faisal was his third son and a direct descendant of Husain the eldest child of Fatima, the favourite daughter of Mohammed, who married the Prophet's adopted son Ali.

Like Mohammed, Faisal had been brought up among the tribesmen of the desert, and although his education was completed in Constantinople he remained at heart a nomad. Before the war he had identified himself with the Arab national movement, but at the outbreak of hostilities had found himself obliged to work for the Turks. He managed to escape to the Hejaz in 1915 where Lawrence encountered him, and it was with and through him that the Revolt in the Desert was carried out.

Writing of Faisal, Lawrence[1] says:

> "He was a man of moods, flickering between glory and despair . . . his dark, appealing eyes, set a little sloping in his face, were bloodshot, and his hollow cheeks deeply lined and puckered with reflection. His nature grudged thinking, for it crippled his speed in action: the labour of it shrivelled his features into swift lines of pain. In appearance he was tall, graceful and vigorous, with the most beautiful gait, and a royal dignity of head and shoulders. Of course he knew it and a great part of his public expression was by sign and gesture.
>
> "His movements were impetuous. He showed himself hot tempered and sensitive, even unreasonable, and he ran off soon on tangents. Appetite and physical weakness were mated in him with the spur of courage. His personal charm, his imprudence, the pathetic hint of frailty as the sole reserve of his proud character made him the idol of his followers. One never asked if he were unscrupulous; but later he showed that he could return trust for trust, suspicion for suspicion. He was fuller of wit than of humour.
>
> "His training in Abdul Hamid's entourage had made him past master in diplomacy. His military service with the Turks

[1] From "Seven Pillars of Wisdom," by T. E. Lawrence, copyright, 1926, 1935, by Doubleday, Doran and Company, Inc.

had given him a working knowledge of tactics. His life in Constantinople and the Turkish parliament had made him familiar with European questions and manners. He was a careful judge of men. If he had the strength to realize his dreams he would go very far, for he was wrapped up in his work and lived for nothing else; but the fear was that he would wear himself out by trying to seem to aim always a little higher than the truth, or that he would die of too much action . . ."

Shortly after General Allenby's entrance into Damascus in October of 1918, a British-sponsored Arab Government was set up which extended as far as Aleppo, with Faisal as its official head. With the support of British troops and the backing of the Iraqui officers, who had served throughout the revolt in the desert, it was intended to establish a federated state of Syria and Iraq. The Paris Peace Conference, however, gave the mandate of Syria to the French, and that of Iraq to the British, so that the project had to be abandoned. This did not exactly suit the Arabs' conception of what Lawrence had suggested would be their reward for their help in the war, and Faisal remained on in Damascus. But the French had no particular regard for Faisal and in 1920 ejected him from Syria with his Arab administrators.

Thus, Gertrude's selection of an Arab king, while not entirely acceptable to the French, suited the circumstances in Iraq, where a man with a great tradition, and at the same time gifts of leadership, was essential.

Before finally making up her mind that this choice was irrevocably the right one, she had, in her usual informal way, talked the matter over with Haji Naji and found that he and his like enthusiastically supported Faisal.

"Let the people do it themselves; the British Government need not interfere!" he replied to Gertrude's question as to whether it would be advisable for the authorities to forcibly back up the Emir's candidature. Quite unofficially then, she began to make use of Haji Naji on behalf of Faisal and when the king-to-be landed in Iraq she sent the old gardener with a *laisser passer* to the British Resident in Basrah. There is probably no record of this visit and the emissary himself was unaware of the importance of his mission, but to Haji Naji is greatly due the reception Faisal met from his future subjects.

It was the Bell touch which never failed when dealing with the Arabs.

The stage, however, was not yet set for the proclaiming of a king. The rivalry between the Sunnis and the Shiahs was becoming more and more bitter. The former were advocating a Turkish prince for the throne on the ground that he would be a better bulwark against the Shiahs than a son of the Sharif. Having the preponderance in the Cabinet, the Sunnis were doing all in their power to give the most important administrative posts, even in Shiah districts, to members of their sect. They could not be made to appreciate that a popular government must have representatives of all the inhabitants, to govern the country.

The Shiahs were so bitter about the turn of events that they made it known that they would prefer a British administration to anything remotely Sunni. Sir Percy and Gertrude had to move warily, knowing that when it came to the point a Moslem would never dare to raise his voice against another Moslem and in favour of an infidel, even if it were the kind of Moslem he despised. Gertrude never lost faith in Faisal as the ideal ruler and to that end she worked regardless of the controversies over his appointment.

In the intervals of kingdom building there were relaxations. Dinner parties at Government House and teas in Gertrude's rose-scented garden when political differences of opinion were forgotten. The greatest social event was a race meeting.

The most important thing in an Arab's life is his horse. Apart from the fact that it is his means of transportation, the Arab loves horses. When one visits an Arab of importance in his home one is not introduced to the family, but to the horses. After whatever meal one has taken, the host calls for the horses and they come flocking round unharnessed and make friends with the guest. A race meeting, therefore, appealed to all the various warring contingents who were trying to run Iraq and for a few days nothing else was thought of.

Sir Percy Cox saw to it that it should all be done on a grand scale, and on "Cup Day" he appeared on the course wearing a frock coat and a grey tall hat which caused a more profound sensation than any speeches about the might of Britain. Gertrude had a new Paris hat and gown and looked as if she were dressed for the Royal Enclosure at Ascot, while the rest of the staff had appropriate costumes.

It must have been a charming spectacle, this small group of English people who were living in constant fear of their lives, dressing in formal clothes and going to the races as if they had no other interests. It must have been an amazing picture to see Baghdadis in their rich robes and austere Shiahs and fanatical Sunnis mixing with the Bedouins of the desert as they made their bets. It must have been the most exciting thing in the world to watch the pure-bred Arab horses flashing round the course mounted by jockeys who had never heard of pulling, and riding to win only.

When the meeting was over Sir Percy made a speech, the Naquib made a speech, Gertrude was called for but said little, and Lady Cox gave away the cups. It was all as peaceful as a summer afternoon in an English village with that same spirit of sportsmanship which exists in the country in England.

However, horse racing could not go on indefinitely, and with the end of the meeting the troubles started again. The new controversy arose over the question as to whether amnesty should be granted to political prisoners and those who had brought about rebellion. Sir Percy was in favour of letting bygones be bygones and starting afresh. This was difficult for the Arabs to understand. Their only conception of ethics in situations of this nature was those based on desert lore. If they raided, they expected to be raided back, and if they had the misfortune to be defeated they could not hope for mercy. Gertrude eventually took the matter in hand and gave a dinner party to all those involved in the controversy. The results were highly successful and the guests parted promising to behave in the future in a brotherly way!

Shortly after this there was a further suspension in state building brought about by the Cairo Conference. Mr. Winston Churchill had just been made Secretary of State for the Colonies and he wanted to obtain first-hand information on what was being done in the Near East.

CHAPTER XV

The new Minister for the Colonies knew the Orient. He was aware that problems in the East were much less complicated than they appeared to the British Cabinet, but impossible to treat as the same kind of situations in Europe. He further realized that at this present juncture, with the nations of the world trying to put President Wilson's ideals into practice, comparatively straightforward questions had to be handled delicately. He accordingly summoned the British representatives from the various countries of the Near East which were going through a process of rebirth, and at the end of February 1921 the conference assembled in Cairo.

Sir Percy Cox was accompanied by Sasun Effendi (the Minister of Finance in the provisional government of Iraq), Jaafar Pasha and Gertrude. Thus after a lapse of six years she found herself once more on the banks of the Nile helping to strengthen the foundations of the British Empire. The problems to be solved by the delegates, in spite of Churchill's optimism, reminded her of a task which a host of Israelites some thousands of years before had carried out on much the same site as this conference. The pyramids remained to prove that the children of Israel had accomplished the impossible and she only hoped that her colleagues would show the same tenacity as the slaves of Pharaoh.

In 1915 Gertrude had been just one of the many called in to advise on her specialized knowledge of Arabia. Now she was one of the most important members of the conference, and the Secretary of Statc would not only listen to her attentively but act on her suggestions.

To the surprise of everyone, among the members of Mr. Churchill's staff was T. E. Lawrence. After the Paris Peace Conference and the repudiation by the governments of the Allies of his promises to the Arabs, Lawrence had retired from public life in disgust. Now he came, sinking his proud personality, to help in the common cause, possibly in the hope of redeeming some of the pledges he had made to his Arab friends. In many ways he succeeded, but when the conference was over and he was offered practically any post at the disposal of the Colonial Office he withdrew again and this time sank his individuality completely by assuming another name and joining the R.A.F. as a private.

Gertrude was pleased to be again with the man who shared her love of the desert and its people, and they once more walked by the Nile where six years previously they had been just Mr. Lawrence and Miss Bell who had solutions to the problems of the Near East which hardly anyone appreciated.

Gertrude's main objective at the Cairo Conference was to have Faisal's candidacy for the throne of Iraq definitely backed by the British Government. Her attitude in this case was definitely feminine. She knew Faisal and she liked him. These factors stood out in his favour before anything else. He was a man with a strong and engaging personality, esteemed by the Arabs, and had done much for the British cause during the war. (Second point in his favour!) But subconsciously dominating her attitude was her dislike for the Minister of the Interior in Baghdad, Saiyid Talib Pasha, son of the Naquib of Basrah. Saiyid was a powerful figure in the Cabinet, and although Gertrude grudgingly admired his abilities she did not trust him. Having settled this opinion of the man and having further decided that Saiyid had personal ambitions, she made up her mind to place every obstacle she could in the way of his attaining them. The easiest was to have someone on the throne who was opposed to his politics. Faisal fulfilled these qualifications and was also the most worthy candidate, so Gertrude applied herself whole-heartedly to the furthering of her scheme. So successful was she in her intriguing that she secured not only the election of her "protégé" but also the exile of Saiyid.

It must not be supposed that in basing her prejudices or instinctive likes and dislikes Gertrude had any ulterior thoughts for her own advancement. No sentiments of this kind ever entered her head, for, though during the succeeding years she was the mainspring of the new régime, she never accepted any honours or rewards herself from the Arabs and remained ever in the background.

The Cairo Conference was successful in its outward results. The candidature of Faisal was approved, his brother the Emir Abdulla was entrusted with the government of Trans-Jordania, a general amnesty was granted and the knotty problem about the future of the Kurds was solved—on paper! The status of the Jews and Arabs in Palestine was also broached and a temporary solution adopted. But one of the most important benefits of the Conference was to enable the Secretary of State to return to England with some understanding of the difficulties which faced the British administrators and he allowed them a freer hand to act as they thought best.

The Conference party reached Baghdad at the beginning of April and, needless to say, found everyone once more at loggerheads. This time it was locally and primarily on the question of the meaning of the words "mandatory" and "mandate." Some interfering newspaper man had seen fit to translate the words in the vernacular press and had given a quite misleading rendering. The expression "mandatory," as introduced by its sponsor Woodrow Wilson, had been explained as "one who undertakes to do a service for another with regards to property placed in his hands by the other" (the "other" being the League of Nations) while "mandate" was "the contract under which the service was performed." In Baghdad the journalist put another sense on "mandatory": "an authoritative requirement as by a sovereign."

The two conceptions were widely different and caused endless misunderstanding. So acute did this misunderstanding become that Gertrude urged Sir Percy to drop the mandatory idea altogether and make the magnificent gesture of drawing up an individual treaty with the Arab State of Iraq. She pointed out that this would sooner or later be demanded by the government in Baghdad and how much better if Britain made the first move. Sir Percy was in agreement with Gertrude, but he knew that the whole question of Iraq was distasteful to the Cabinet in England and he must not try experiments with anything which had not already been agreed upon.

There was trouble too on the frontiers of Iraq. The Bolshevik Russians, whose foreign policy differed in no way from that of the Tsarist, had their eyes on North Persia and it seemed likely that they might occupy that territory with a view to dominating the whole of the Near East. The Turks were also doing all they could to undermine British influence and excite the extremist Nationalists to assert themselves. The only possible way to avert a return to chaos was to have a ruler in Iraq whose authority would be unquestionable.

Unfortunately the statement on British policy in the Near East, which should have been made in the House of Commons by Winston Churchill on his return from Cairo, was considered sufficiently unimportant to be postponed several times, and it was not until May 13th that the pronouncement was made.

As soon as the attitude of Great Britain to the claimant to the throne of Iraq was officially known, Faisal took action. On June 22nd he sent a wireless to the Naquib announcing his imminent arrival in Basrah, and Baghdad made ready to receive him. The city was at once plunged into turmoil, no one quite knowing how a future king should be welcomed! Then someone thought of Gertrude and she was sought out to solve the conundrum.

Hoping to avoid this further responsibility she formed a reception committee which proved itself quite incompetent. Where would Faisal be lodged? No one had the smallest idea. Should he come up to Baghdad by boat or by train? A terrific controversy which almost ended in blows. Would it be right to have a guard of honour to meet him? Much doubt in the minds of the members of the committee as to what constituted a guard of honour. The final question baffled the clearest thinkers. How about a national flag? The country had none . . .

Gertrude attended the first meeting of the reception committee and, realizing that it would be more of a hindrance than a help, left it to argue and went about arranging the details herself. She called on the railway officials and had a special train made up to fetch Faisal from Basrah. The only suitable place she could think of in which to lodge the Emir was the old government offices, at that time in a state of disrepair. Gertrude approached the Public Works Department, which was about as efficient an organization as the reception committee, and demanded action. This was merely a formality and, having received the vague replies she anticipated, she set out for the bazaar. She had the notables produce costly carpets for the floors of the Emir's residence and rich hangings for the walls; she had the merchants find furniture and crockery and silver, she delegated Fattuh to collect suitable and competent servants. She then went home and designed a temporary flag for Iraq and had it made up. She superintended the drilling of the guard of honour, dismissed the reception committee, which was still arguing frenziedly, and then went to bed.

On June 23rd Faisal arrived in Basrah and was accorded a splendid welcome. Sir Percy and Gertrude felt relieved and, in a lesser state of tension, waited for the Emir's move to Baghdad. There was some little delay on the programme as scheduled, for, like all Orientals to whom dates are merely convenient means of remembering historical events, he thought nothing of spending a day here and a day there on his way north, so that it was not until June 29th that the official arrival was announced.

At six in the morning the town was seething with sightseers, the walls of the houses were decorated with lovely carpets and Gertrude's Sharifian flag flew at every possible point. At six-thirty the notables began to arrive at the station in reversed seniority and were followed by the Cabinet. At seven, Sir Percy Cox and Gertrude, with the staff, motored up in their ceremonial dress. The guard of honour successfully presented arms; there was a general shaking of hands and then a breathless wait. The greatest moment in the history of Iraq was approaching—but nothing happened. The sun became hotter and hotter, the Europeans damper and damper, the talk more and more strained, and then came a message that there had been a landslide on the railway and a rumour that the Emir was coming by motor car!

The feeling of anticlimax became tinged with Oriental fatalism. Sir Percy greeted those whom he had omitted to handshake before, the staff made conversation and Gertrude tried to keep a straight face.

The sun rose higher and higher and the heat became intolerable. Then another message. The landslide had been cleared away and Faisal would arrive in his train at noon. Sir Percy briskly took command. The middle of a June day in Baghdad is an unfit time for any member of the human race to be out of doors. A message was accordingly sent to Faisal asking him to wait in his train until the evening and make his arrival at six P.M. The High Commissioner, the Cabinet and the notables then drove back to their residences through crowds buzzing with contradictory rumours.

At five-thirty that evening the same procedure as in the morning was observed. Flags, guards of honour, handshaking, uniforms, and Gertrude on tenterhooks lest any other contretemps should arise. The hour of six approached and then, to everyone's relief, the train was heard wheezing over the desert.

As the engine creaked to a standstill at the platform, Faisal was seen, tall and magnificent in his robes, standing at the carriage door. The guard of honour presented arms, Faisal saluted, the dignitaries applauded and Sir Percy advanced and shook the Emir's hand. Gertrude kept herself in the background, but Faisal was looking for her and, going to her, took both her hands in silent greeting which said more than all the speeches and all the cheers.

Similarly, on the day following the reception, when Gertrude had gone to Faisal's quarters to leave an official card the Emir heard that she was there and at once sent an A.D.C. to call her in. As she entered his apartments he once more grasped both her hands and, with emotion in his voice, said:

"I couldn't have believed that you could have given me so much help as you have given me."

For a while they sat side by side talking, Faisal telling Gertrude that, as long as she remained, no harm could come to Iraq. As she said goodbye, he added:

"Wherever I go, the people ask: Is Miss Bell satisfied?"

The official receptions and interchange of visits culminated with a banquet held in the Maude Gardens. The place was lit with coloured lanterns, concealed musicians played softly in the warm darkness as rare dishes were served to the guests reclining on rich carpets. After the meal the most distinguished poets of Baghdad recited odes in honour of the Emir. It was a picture straight out of the Arabian Nights, an atmosphere of peace of long ago with all political differences of opinion forgotten . . .

But there were differences of opinion, masses of them. The tribes of the lower Euphrates were not sure that they wanted a king and there were plenty of discontents to fan ill-feeling in the cities. Gertrude and Sir Percy knew that these troublemakers were in the minority and that once Faisal was proclaimed king they would fade away. His bearing and personality had already captured the imagination of all those in Baghdad, regardless of sect or creed. The problem was how to get the election over quickly. It would take at least two months to obtain a referendum from the whole country, and anything, including a change of policy in England, might occur during that period.

It was the Naquib who took the matter into his own hands and on July 11th proposed a resolution to the Council of Ministers, which was unanimously approved, that the Emir Faisal should be declared king without the formalities of a general election. It was a simple Oriental way of dealing with a complicated situation and Sir Percy was delighted at this turn of events. At the same time he had to remember that he was responsible to a Cabinet of Occidental-minded ministers in England and an official proclamation could not be made until the referendum had been taken. However, Faisal was now, to all intents and purposes, king and the setting in motion of the machinery to have him elected by the people had become a formality.

The Naquib gave another Arabian Nights banquet to celebrate this decision in his own palace opposite the mosque. The town was completely illuminated and ancient coloured lanterns hung from innumerable minarets. Crowds jammed the entrance to the house, cheering the guests as they arrived.

The main dinner table had been placed on the long gallery, above the courtyard in which were seated about a hundred minor guests. When the Emir arrived the Naquib rose and kissed him on both cheeks, leading him then to the place of honour opposite him, with the commander-in-chief on one side and Gertrude on the other. It was a spectacle entirely remote from the twentieth century and impossible to associate with Leagues of Nations and mandates, though perhaps it fitted into the idealistic tempo of Mr. Wilson's dreams of self-determined nations! There were no speeches and the guests simply enjoyed themselves, disregarding the fact that they were making history.

Entertainments now followed one another in quick succession, which was trying, with the thermometer standing well over a hundred at night. The Coxes gave a huge party and one evening Gertrude accompanied Faisal to dine with the Jews. There was a certain amount of apprehension as to the outcome of this meeting. An Arab Government might mean disaster for the Jewish element in Iraq; but no sooner had Faisal crossed his host's threshold and made it clear by his friendly attitude that the Jews would have nothing to fear, than the tension was relieved . . .

The leading Rabbi, in his turban and twisted shawl, offered Faisal the Rolls of the Law in their golden cylinders, which he kissed, and then presented him with a gold facsimile of the Law and a beautifully bound Talmud. Faisal then spoke, and his charming dignity at once held the assembly, and when he insisted that the Jews and the Arabs were of the same race, an audible sigh of relief went round the building. Faisal talked to many of those present at the party and when he left he had gained the support of every Jew in Baghdad.

In the intervals of feasting there was practical work to be done. New laws to be drafted, proclamations to be prepared and, curiously enough, the instruction of Faisal in the geography of Iraq!

As a matter of fact this was not quite as peculiar as might be supposed. Mesopotamia had been under the traditional sovereignty of the Sharifian family for centuries, but Faisal had spent most of his life in Arabia and knew less of Iraq than a Bengali might know of the Punjab. The country and its new boundaries had come into being as a separate State during the war and, as Gertrude had been greatly responsible for its creation, it was she who was deputed to teach the new king about his frontiers.

The most dramatic function of all the proclamation ceremonies was the swearing allegiance to Faisal by the desert people. The spot chosen for the rite was Ramadi on the Euphrates, the headquarters of Ali Sulaiman, the Sheik of the Dulaim. From before daybreak, crowds of tribal horsemen, in their flowing robes and fully armed, waited for miles on either side of the road. The villages and oases were decorated with brightly-coloured carpets and as Faisal moved slowly along towards the black ceremonial tent pitched in the desert, the mounted warriors galloped about firing their rifles and shouting wildly in incredible clouds of dust.

Below the steep edge of the Syrian desert were drawn up the fighting men of the Anazeh tribes, afoot and on horseback, accompanied by camel riders bearing their chiefs' standards. The great tent, two hundred feet long with a dais at one end and walled with palm branches, stood on the bank of the Euphrates. Outside the tent were drawn up more horsemen and negro standard-bearers on gigantic white camels.

Faisal, majestic in his robes, with a black abba and his turban bound with strands of silver cord, walked with dignity to the dais and sat down. On his right was Fahad Bey, the paramount Sheik of Amarah; on his left, Gertrude Bell. As he settled himself in his seat and looked down on the chiefs before him, his face lit up with a smile which expressed happiness and confidence. In Baghdad he was still a curiosity and had to be watchful about breaches of etiquette, but here he was among his own desert people whom he understood and who would understand what he had to say. For a moment he paused, savouring the silence; then, in the sonorous, magnificent tongue of the desert he began to speak as a tribal chief to his feudatories.

"For four years I have not found myself in a place like this or in such company," he began, and paused again as the pride in his voice sent murmurs of approval round the huge tent.

He then went on to tell the chiefs of the future of Iraq with him at its head, and, raising his voice at the conclusion of the speech, cried:

"O Arabs, are you at peace with one another?"

"Yes, yes, we are at peace!" they shouted as one man.

"From this date and from this hour of the morning,"

Faisal continued in ringing tones, "any tribesman who lifts a hand against a tribesman is responsible to me—I will be your judge . . . I have my rights over you as your Lord."

A grey-bearded old sheik interrupted:

"And our rights?"

"And you have your rights as subjects which it is my business to guard!" he replied.

"Yes, yes, the truth by Allah, yes, by Allah!" shouted the chiefs, making the desert re-echo as the nomads outside took up the cry. It was magnificent, a tribal gathering of the old, old days long before Islam and the Prophet.

When the cheering had died down Ali Sulaiman and Fahad Bey rose and said slowly:

"We swear allegiance to you because you are acceptable to the British Government."

Faisal looked up with a momentary expression of surprise and then, smiling at Gertrude, replied:

"No one can doubt what my relations are to the British . . . but we must settle our affairs ourselves."

He looked again at Gertrude who clasped her two hands together as a symbol of the union between the Arabs and the British. There was a moment of complete silence and then a tremendous shout of approval which was once more taken up by the tribesmen outside the tent.

Gertrude closed her eyes, feeling that tears would be the only relief to the emotions which welled up in her at finding all that she had dreamed of and worked for, against such odds, had been realized . . .

For the next hour the sheiks approached Faisal in turn and, laying their hands in his, swore allegiance.

In the afternoon followed the rite of swearing allegiance

by the villages and oases. From the whole width and breadth of Iraq all the Mayors and Qazis and notables had gathered by the Euphrates. The ceremony took place in the palm-shaded greenness of an oasis. A lofty dais had been erected against a blank wall draped with carpets. Faisal took his place on the dais with Gertrude, while the notables sat in rows beneath. As each one's turn came he walked slowly up and laid his hands in those of the Emir with the same ritual as observed by the Bedouins. The atmosphere was perhaps not as dramatic as at the ceremony of the morning, but it was very beautiful. There was much more colour . . . the green of the feathery palm trees, the red kerchiefs of the elders, the bright carpets, the white turbans and, above it all, the immense dignity of Faisal.

As Gertrude rode back with him and his suite through the gardens of the oasis to find their lodging, everyone paid as much respect to the English-woman as to the Emir. Fahad Bey watched the salutations with a satisfied smile and said:

"One of the reasons why you stand out is because you are a woman. There is only one Miss Bell. It is like when Sidi Faisal was in London and wore his Arab dress, there was no one like him; so for a hundred years they will talk of Miss Bell riding by."

CHAPTER XVI

By the end of August 1921 the results of the people of Iraq's referendum were known and Faisal had the satisfaction of hearing that ninety-six per cent of his subjects had voted for him. The only opposition to his election came from the unimportant Turkoman and Kurdish communities in the Kirkik district.

The voters were rather puzzled at the necessity of an election, having been accustomed to wake up any morning and find a new ruler who had taken possession of the country overnight. Political slogans completely baffled the great majority of the constituents, especially the meaning of democracy which did not seem to fit in with tribal life.

Gertrude was one day waiting in the anteroom of the Prime Minister's house and overheard a sheik from Hayil trying to have this expression made clear to him.

The Naquib: Are you a Damakrati?

The Sheik: No, I'm not a Magrati, what is it?

The Naquib: Well, I am the Sheik of the Damakratiyah!

The Sheik (evidently feeling that there must be some misunderstanding): Allah, I take refuge in God. If you are the Sheik of Makratiyah, then I must be one of them, for I am altogether at your service. (Pause.) But what is it?

The Naquib: Damakratiyah is equality, there is no big man and no little. All are equal.

The Sheik (in consternation at the thought of his tribal authority slipping from him through this new-fangled idea): God is my witness, if that's it I'm not a Magrati! . . .

As a matter of fact, no one really cared what outward form the government took. All that the tribesmen and townspeople wanted was peace and prosperity after the turmoils of war. Faisal appealed to them by his name and personality; they knew that the British were behind him, and Gertrude advocated his candidature for the throne: so they elected him.

On Tuesday August 23, 1921, Faisal al Husain was crowned King of Iraq.

In the centre of the great courtyard of the government buildings a dais had been erected. Priceless carpets hung from all the windows and strewed the paving. On either side of the dais a guard of honour of the Dorsetshire Regiment in full dress was drawn up, and crowding into the rest of the courtyard were deputations of chiefs and notables from all over the country in their picturesque robes. It was just after sunrise and the air still had a little of the flower-scented coolness of the night.

As the sun sent its first burning rays into the courtyard Sir Percy in uniform, his breast glittering with decorations, followed by the members of his staff, paced down the path of rich carpets. Faisal, dignified but evidently undergoing a great mental strain, walked beside the High Commissioner. He anxiously scanned the rows of privileged guests and, seeing Gertrude, gave her an almost imperceptible nod which she returned with a smile of encouragement.

As soon as the royal party was established on the dais, the Naquib's son stood up and read the proclamation which announced that ninety-six per cent of the population of Iraq had elected Faisal their King. Everyone in the assembly rose to his feet to salute the new monarch with a cry of: "Long live the King!" The band of the Dorsetshires struck up "God Save the King" as Gertrude, having neglected her music studies in her youth, had found it impossible to compose an Iraqui national anthem, and her famous flag was broken at the flagstaff, while guns boomed twenty-one times over the sluggish waters of the Tigris.

Sir Percy then read out the decree announcing that His Britannic Majesty recognized the Emir Faisal as the rightful King of Iraq. He was followed by the aged Naquib who respectfully tendered his resignation and that of the Cabinet. Faisal held the hands of the Prime Minister to whom he owed so much and begged him to remain in office. The Naquib bowed and was about to retire when Sir Percy stopped him. Laying the blade of his sword on the old man's shoulder, he made it known that, in recognition of his invaluable services to his country and the wise counsel which he had given to Britain's representatives in Iraq, His Majesty King George V had been pleased to confer on him the high distinction of Knight Grand Commander of the British Empire. There was a great cheer; and the historic ceremony, superb in its simplicity, was over.

Gertrude and Sir Percy walked to their waiting car through the lines of delighted Baghdadis, smiling their responses to the congratulations being expressed on all sides and genuinely relieved that the main goal of their enterprise had been reached. As they parted Gertrude remarked, almost to herself:

"This is the last time I engage in king-making, it's too great a strain."

Truly a tremendous strain and one which was not yet over, for, like the stone of Sisyphus which always rolled back from the top of the hill, it seemed as if it only needed matters to become settled in Iraq for everything to be more unsettled than before.

Apart from all the intricate details of forming a representative government, introducing a parliamentary system and settling frontier disputes, there was still the all important and unsettled question of the national flag and royal standard! Gertrude took her flag making as seriously as her other administrative duties! She designed and undesigned and finally wrote to her father for his advice:

> ". . . Father, do for Heaven's sake say," she wrote, "whether the Hejaz[1] flag is heraldically right. You might telegraph. It's a very good flag and we could differentiate it from the Iraq by putting a gold star on the black stripe or on the red triangle. Do let me know before the congress meets. Also whether you have a better idea for the Faisal standard . . ."

The vital necessity of this flag might have seemed exaggerated to those who did not know the Arabs as well as Gertrude. But she realized that the tribal standard had always been an emblem of unity and represented the authority of sheiks and their families. If, therefore, the people of Iraq were to live henceforward as one people under one paramount sheik, there must be a national flag, or single

[1] A small independent country ruled over by Ibn Saud, but important as including within its frontiers the holy cities of Mecca and Medina and the pilgrim port of Jidda.

tribal standard, which would be more important than the local banners.

That Gertrude was right in her views on this subject became more apparent as the problems of the outlying districts of Iraq become more acute.

While there was a stable government in Baghdad and the immediate vicinity, the frontiers of the new State and the neighbouring countries were still in turmoil. The Kurds still had leanings towards the Turks and it was easy for Turkish propagandists to stir up strife. To the southwest, Ibn Saud had taken possession of Hayil and become aggressive, permitting raids into the tribal areas ruled by Faisal. Eventually Sir Percy Cox decided that action was the only thing which dissidents understood. This action was greatly facilitated by the putting into force of a measure, decided on principle at the Cairo Conference, that all the troops in Iraq should be under the supervision of the Royal Air Force. Air Marshal Sir John Salmond took over command in October of 1922 and began immediately to vigorously oppose any sign of rebellion. On the smallest provocation air raids were instituted with the result that in a few months the Turkish propagandists disappeared and the warring tribesmen returned to their pastures. The extremist Nationalists in Baghdad, however, seized the opportunity to suggest that the insurrections and the subsequent raids had been instituted to make Iraq realize the extent of its dependence on Great Britain.

The atmosphere was highly charged and it looked as if the work carried out by Gertrude and Sir Percy Cox would, after all, come to nothing. The King and his ministers went about their business as if everything was running smoothly, but the feeling was one of restless uncertainty.

The crisis came on the first anniversary of the King's accession. It was a stifling August morning when Gertrude, wearing for the first time all her war medals and decorations on a lace dress, accompanied Sir Percy to the palace. They found the courtyard packed with a crowd of white-robed people who remained sulkily silent and without a sign of recognition when the High Commissioner arrived. Before, however, he could make any comment to Gertrude, he found himself surrounded by policemen who had practically to clear a passage through the sullen multitude. As he made his way up the palace staircase a voice shouted something insulting and was followed by applause and boos. Sir Percy took no notice and went into the audience chamber where he found the King looking nervous and ill at ease. Still maintaining an attitude of being unaware of anything untoward, Sir Percy offered his formal congratulations and left with his staff.

As soon as they reached Government House, Sir Percy took Gertrude aside and told her to find out what had occurred outside the palace. In an hour Gertrude came back with the information that the crowd in question was composed of Nationalists who had staged an anti-British, anti-mandate demonstration. She added that this was but a preliminary of worse to come.

Sir Percy was very angry but he said nothing, and took no further action that day. He waited until the anniversary celebrations were over, and early the next morning called at the palace. He found the household in an atmosphere of chaos. During the night the King had had a severe attack of appendicitis and two English and three Arab doctors were about to operate. It was the most critical moment in the history of Iraq and any weakness when the ruler might be on his deathbed could bring disaster.

Sir Percy acted with his usual promptness and forcefulness. He at once issued a proclamation explaining the situation and calling on all persons who had the welfare of the country at heart to rally round the High Commissioner and resist any form of violence on the part of the extremists. At the same time the revolutionary ringleaders were arrested, no meetings were allowed and certain seditious newspapers were suppressed. Simultaneously, two holy men from Persia who had had much to do with the anti-British, anti-mandate demonstrations were advised to take a holiday if they valued the good state of their health. In the interior of Iraq all Arab officials suspected of sympathizing with the revolutionaries were dismissed or transferred to other posts.

The effect of these measures was instantaneous, and, by the beginning of September, the whole of Iraq was quiet. As soon as the King was convalescent, he received Sir Percy and publicly thanked him for the action which had been taken while he was ill.

The atmosphere was further cleared by an announcement by Winston Churchill that the mandate would end the day Iraq was admitted to the League of Nations.

The autumn and winter came and went in tranquillity. Gertrude was able to give more time to her archaeology and continue her collecting for the Baghdad Museum. C. L. Woolley, no longer in uniform, appeared in Iraq as head of a mission sent out by the British Museum and Pennsylvania University, and became Gertrude's friendly collaborator in spite of the fact that he was collecting for a rival museum. The Baghdadis had had their excitement, the tribesmen had scented war and, realizing that Sir Percy never threatened without the intention of carrying out his threats, decided that it was better policy to keep quiet. Actually the great majority of the people of Iraq genuinely wanted to work. For years their agriculture and commerce had practically ceased to function because of inter-tribal strife, and there was a great deal of poverty and want. No one realized this more than Faisal and his two faithful British friends, and together they set to work to remedy the ravages of years of strife.

Sir Percy's duties were naturally concentrated on the official administration of the country and it fell to Gertrude to handle the more personal aspect of the national problems. In this she found an ally and friend in the King; and an understanding intimacy, probably unprecedented between an Occidental woman and an Oriental man, developed between the two collaborators. Their trains of thought followed such similar lines that it was almost impossible to believe that Faisal had not had the British upbringing and the Oxford education of Gertrude.

If the King had a knotty problem to solve, he would call Gertrude over to the palace for a cup of tea and discuss what he had in his mind as informally as if he had been with his family. In the early morning he would ride with Gertrude among the gardens of the oasis and sometimes make a surprise call on Haji Naji or some other landowner. There would be more informal talking over tea, and splendid propaganda made for the King among the humbler citizens of Baghdad. In the evening Gertrude would often be asked to drop in at the palace for a game of bridge. Faisal was a good player, but his ministers were not; so Gertrude undertook bridge classes, which were taken as seriously as the affairs of state. When Faisal built an annex to his palace he was in perplexity as to how to furnish it. Gertrude was summoned. She examined the room, suggested sofas and comfortable armchairs and, receiving the King's approval, sent to England for the kind of furniture associated with smoking rooms in a London club.

One evening Gertrude gave a picnic bathing party by moonlight to which Faisal came. She brought out carpets and cushions and hung Baghdad lanterns in the tamarisk bushes. After a swim in the mysterious half-light of a young moon the party returned to the cushions and roasted fish on spits over a fire of palm branches and drank coffee and talked. Then, gradually the conversation died away as the hostess and her guests lay back contentedly and let their minds wander, to the lullaby of the Tigris lapping the banks of the oasis.

"This is peace," murmured the King, and there was no one to contradict him.

When things had been going quietly for some little time, Gertrude suggested to Sir Percy that he give a garden party and include among his guests all those who had caused trouble. Sir Percy was amused at Gertrude's audacity, but he approved the plan; and the party was held on the King's birthday, with all the officials and nobles and prominent citizens bidden to attend, regardless of their political convictions. No one refused the invitation. Gertrude took personal charge of the King and saw to it that he had a word with everyone. The whole affair was a huge success and the party broke up with the most violent antagonists hobnobbing as if they had never had a difference of opinion in their lives.

Gertrude had that uncanny instinct with Orientals which made it possible for her to do things which other Occidentals, who had spent years in the East, could not attempt. She never approached that state which is referred to as "going native," and while not offending traditions or customs, she treated them in a practical way.

Again and again she would find herself faced with situations which required unhesitating action. Sometimes they were matters of political importance, sometimes simple incidents of daily life. But she met each and every contingency with an alert mind which out-thought those of the other parties concerned.

She was breakfasting one morning in one of the gardens of the oasis with Haji Naji, when an unpleasant looking Dervish strode into the summer-house where the meal was laid and announced that he had come as a guest. Gertrude's host told the man to go away. The only reply was a lot of blustering and a statement to the effect that he had as much right to share breakfast as the infidel woman. The host called to his servants and ordered them to remove the Dervish; but before hands could be laid on him he had sat down outside the summer-house and, taking a Koran from out of his robes, begun to read aloud. The breakfast-giver was in a quandary. The Dervish was being a nuisance, but, as long as he sat reading the Koran, his action must be regarded as a blessing and he could not be moved.

Gertrude had resented being referred to as a female infidel, and for a while she said nothing, but when the man's reading became so loud that she could not hear herself speak she got up and told the reader to be gone! The man replied:

"I am reading the Koran."

"I can hear you are," retorted Gertrude sarcastically, "and if you don't stop immediately and go away, I shall send for the police!"

"I rely on God," answered the man irrelevantly.

"God is a long way off and the police are very near," said Gertrude acidly.

The man pretended he had not heard this blasphemy and went on reading his Koran, so Gertrude picked up his staff and poked him in the ribs. The Dervish stared in amazement at this extraordinary female who blasphemed and then assaulted one of God's elect, but there was no mistaking her future intentions as to his person; so he got up and meekly went on his way, and Gertrude never heard another word about the incident.

Gertrude was now fifty-three, so she decided that it was time to take up flying.

Flying in the desert presents great dangers. There are, to begin with, unpleasant air pockets; and secondly, almost certainty of dying of thirst and starvation if one is forced to land anywhere which is not within sight of a caravan track. But these risks did not worry Gertrude; riding to Hayil had not bothered her, so why should flying?

Her first long flight was to see her father. They had not met for some time, and as he could not come all the way to Baghdad Gertrude suggested a rendezvous in Jerusalem. All plans were made and at nine one morning, accompanied by a British military plane, she started on her flight. Sir Hugh Bell drove out to the aerodrome and soon two specks appeared in the eastern sky. Before one o'clock Gertrude had made a perfect landing and was in her father's arms.

That night she put on a new frock, which Sir Hugh had brought out from England, and went to dinner with Faisal's brother, the Emir of Transjordan.

A fortnight later she flew back to Baghdad, declaring that airplanes were the only sensible method of transportation in the desert!

The political situation in Iraq, though more settled, was not all that Sir Percy had hoped for. He was all the more disappointed as his term of office was coming to an end and he wanted to retire with a feeling that something permanent had been accomplished. One of the main problems which still faced the High Commissioner was the Turkish propaganda which based itself chiefly on a rumour that Iraq was to be returned to Turkey. This rumour was given strength by the conciliatory attitude of the Allied Powers at the Lausanne Conference.

Sir Percy felt that the government of Iraq must take a more vigorous line of action to meet these emergencies, and the Naquib was no longer the right man to hold the all-important position of Prime Minister. He was getting very old and could hardly walk unassisted. Gertrude had several confidential talks with him and was able to convey to Sir Percy that the aged man would be glad to resign. The resignation was, accordingly, arranged without friction or ill-feeling, and a younger and more vigorous man, Abdul Muhsin Bey, became Premier and at once reconstructed the Cabinet.

This problem solved, another complication presented itself with a change of government in England in which there was a large faction which still favoured the evacuation of all Near Eastern mandates by the British.

Luckily for Iraq, Sir Percy was able to go to England at the beginning of 1923 and take part in the discussions about the future of the country. His eloquence on behalf of King Faisal and his insistence that it was imperative not to alter existing conditions were successful, and he returned to Baghdad in March with a new treaty. The new treaty pleased the Iraquis, as it reduced the maintenance of the original military and commercial agreements between the two countries from a period of twenty years to four, with a stipulation that it could be renewed or abrogated or changed if it was thought advisable by both signatories.

The ratification of this treaty by the High Commissioner and the Prime Minister was Sir Percy Cox's last official act in Iraq, and early in May he left the country for good.

Sir Percy's departure created an irreparable blank in Gertrude's life. She had been working with him for over six years, not so much as one of his official staff but as a confidential collaborator. When she joined him in 1916 he had already spent thirty years in the Orient as a political officer, and there was little he did not know about Persia and Mesopotamia. Gertrude had not been so long in the East, but she was an expert on the subject and knew it from a different point of view than that of the High Commissioner. Whereas Sir Percy was a government servant who, by force of circumstances, had been obliged to deal with people and situations officially, Gertrude saw the countries and their inhabitants from another angle. There could not have been a better combination of two people in harness working for a common end, and it is doubtful whether the results achieved would have been possible without this team.

Throughout the harassing years of war when defeat threatened the British forces in Mesopotamia, and during the anxious period of peace-making, Gertrude and Sir Percy had but one objective: the creation of an Arab kingdom. When this was finally achieved and Sir Percy reluctantly went into retirement, Gertrude felt as if some physical part of herself had been torn away.

As Sir Percy and Gertrude drove from Government House to the Station, on the morning of the High Commissioner's departure, they made no attempt at conversation. The houses were decorated and throngs of silent people lined the familiar streets. On the platform were all the officials in Baghdad and a number of desert chiefs, and, though the Arab is not given to tears, there were many who had a tight feeling about their throats as they shook hands with the man who had stood by them during their years of travail.

Sir Percy entered the train, the signal of its departure was given and slowly it went creaking over the desert while Gertrude stood with blurred eyes, oblivious of all those about her.

CHAPTER XVII

Sir Henry Dobbs, who succeeded Sir Percy Cox as High Commissioner, had been Counsellor at Government House for over a year. He knew the country and its problems and had been a colleague of Sir Percy during the war. Most of his previous official service had been in India. Sir Henry and Gertrude knew each other well and held each other in high esteem. It was, nevertheless, a change of régime, and, although Gertrude felt that she could never completely divorce herself from the country which she had made her home, she did not want to cling to a post merely because she had held it for some time. Her actual task in the making of Irāq into a kingdom was finished, but her advice and assistance in handling the Arabs could still be of great value, and physically she did not suggest her years.

Marguerite Harrison, writing in the *New York Times*, said of Gertrude:

"When I was first in Baghdad in 1923 I had the privilege of seeing Gertrude Bell on many occasions. The first time that I met her was by appointment at her office. After waiting for a few moments I was ushered into a small room with a high ceiling and long French windows facing the river. It was the untidiest room I have ever seen, chairs, tables and sofas being littered with documents, maps, pamphlets and papers. At a desk piled high with documents that had overflowed onto the carpet sat a slender woman in a smart frock of knitted silk. As she rose I noticed that her figure was still willowy and graceful. Her delicate oval face with its firm mouth and chin and steel blue eyes and with its aureole of soft grey hair, was the face of a 'grande dame.' There was nothing of the weather-beaten hardened explorer in her looks or bearing. 'Paris frock, Mayfair manners.' And this was the woman who had made sheiks tremble at the thought of the 'Anglez'!

"Her smile was completely disarming, as was the gesture with which she swept all the papers from the sofa to the floor to make room for me . . ."

As it happened, everything worked out serenely for Gertrude. The High Commissioner asked her to stay on in Baghdad in an advisory capacity, and the King, in whom Lawrence had inspired a genuine interest in the study of antiquities, appointed her honorary director of archaeology with a mission to create for Baghdad a fine museum. No one was better qualified for this task than Gertrude, who even in the midst of the political turmoils had kept up her interest in the ruins and excavations round Baghdad.

Neither need Gertrude have had any worries as to Sir Henry Dobbs' appreciation of her abilities. In his first confidential report on the members of his staff which he sent to the British Government he said about her:

"It is difficult to write of Miss Bell's services both to the British and Iraq Governments without seeming to exaggerate. Her remarkable knowledge of this country and its people and her sympathy with them enable her to penetrate into their minds, while her inextinguishable faith prevents her from being discouraged by what she sometimes finds there. Her long acquaintance with the tribes and sheiks makes her advice in the recurring crisis in tribal affairs invaluable and her vitality and width of culture make her house a focus for all that is worth having in both European and Arab society in Baghdad. She is, in fact, the connecting link between the British and Arab races without which there would be dislocation both of public business and of private amenities."

To Gertrude's satisfaction and relief, Sir Henry showed that he had every intention of carrying on Sir Percy Cox's policy of firmness with the discontents and propagandists.

His first act was to move a mixed force of British and Iraqui troops to Mosul. That Mosul should be embodied in the mandatory area was of paramount importance. In addition to being a strategic point vital to Iraq in a military way (the Zagros mountain system in which it lay forming an impregnable protective zone to the whole of the Tigris and Euphrates valleys), it was commercially invaluable. It was a tremendous grain growing centre and a wool market, but above all it held one of the richest oil fields of the world. Great Britain could not afford to let this oil fall into other hands, and the British delegation in Geneva was entirely in accord with Sir Henry Dobbs over the question of Mosul, which gave him a free hand in handling the problems in this part of the country.

Often when Gertrude was drawing up reports about the Mosul oil fields her mind wandered back to those carefree days, long ago, when on her way to Tehran to stay with her uncle she had been taken to see the "Naphtha Springs" near Batoum which were exploited at such a loss! Now, with the passage of barely thirty years, this oil, which had been made use of by the people of Nineveh two thousand years before Christ, was important enough for Britain to risk the rekindling of war in the Near East.

The mixed force dispatched by Sir Henry camped on the site of Nineveh on the opposite side of the Tigris to Mosul and was joined by units of the Royal Air Force. Turkish irregulars, with the co-operation of the Sheik Mahmud of Sulaimanya, were planning a Kurdish uprising. The Anglo-Iraqui troops, supported by the airplanes, advanced into enemy territory; and after one or two skirmishes and some effective bombing the Sheik fled, the Turkish trouble-makers disappeared and the Mosul border returned to tranquillity.

Sir Henry then turned his attention to the discontents in Baghdad. The underlying causes of trouble were, as usual, the Shiah elders, who were doing all they could to make their influence felt in the elections of the new Constituent Assembly. The chief agitator was a certain Sheik Mahdi al Khalisi, a traditionally powerful leader throughout all districts where the Shiah element predominated. Sir Henry knew that, until this man had been put out of the way, there would be no peace. At the same time, it would be an exceedingly delicate matter for a member of an "infidel" race to lay hands on a person of such reputed sanctity among Moslems. At Gertrude's suggestion, therefore, the King was approached and told that the unpleasant task must be his. Faisal at once understood, and the tiresome Sheik Mahdi was deported by exclusive Arab agency. This deportation had the unexpected, but gratifying, effect of causing several other prominent Persian divines to leave the country as a public protest. Sir Henry waited until they were over the border and then quickly forbade their return until after the elections.

As a result of these decisive measures on the frontier and in Baghdad, the agitators realized that a change of High Commissioner had not altered the British policy in Iraq, and the political atmosphere cleared rapidly. By the end of the year the enormous task of registering the electors had been completed.

This was preceded by a reshuffling of the Cabinet, the resignation of Abdul Muhsin Bey, and the appointment of Jaafar Pasha as Prime Minister.

Gertrude, seeing that all Sir Percy's projects were being carried through by his successor, allowed herself some relaxation. She continued giving her advice when it was required and kept in touch with what was going on behind the scenes, but she could now find more time for less nerve-straining pursuits.

Always devoted to horses and anything related to them, she felt that they might be the means of bringing the British and the Arabs closer together. The famous race meeting in those days of tension had shown how political differences could be forgotten when horses held the first place. So she suggested the formation of Arab polo teams, and found in the officers of the Inniskilling Fusiliers, now stationed in Baghdad, eager abettors in her scheme; and in the autumn of 1923 she inaugurated the first Arab-British polo match. The success of these matches was not entirely unqualified, for, whereas the Arabs were superb horsemen, they had a certain difficulty in assimilating the rules and could see no reason why a game should not go on indefinitely until one of the sides gave in from exhaustion. However, polo did have the desired effect of bringing the Englishmen and the people of Iraq into the kind of relationship which would have been impossible otherwise.

She took up Mah Jong and found the Arab ministers much apter pupils at this game than at bridge, and in a short time her house was a gay centre of enthusiastic Mah

Jong parties. One evening a British officer of the staff, with musical tastes, thought it might be a good idea to treat the Arabs to a sample of Occidental music. A piano was produced around which was gathered a solemn audience of desert chiefs. The Englishman, equally solemn, sat before the piano and played the "Sonata Pathétique." The last chords died away to the dignified silence of a polite people who have the same feelings about European music as Europeans have about Arab. But when Gertrude requested an opinion the verdict was unanimous: "Wallahi! Khosh daggah!" (By God! A good thumping!)

Lady Dobbs arrived towards the end of the year from England and was given an enthusiastic reception, and social life at Government House soon became a feature in Baghdad. Gertrude was glad to have another woman with whom she could forget treaties and politics and Moslem problems. She had great ability for concealing the fact that she had the ablest brain in the mandate organization, and could fit herself when necessary into the description of her in the *New York Times:* "Paris frock and Mayfair manners." A strange woman whom the females treated as a female and the males as a male or a female, according to the mood of the moment.

One of the first official parties which Sir Henry Dobbs gave was to the King and his Cabinet and the British heads of departments in the mandatory organization. Gertrude received an invitation, but before accepting she gave the matter a little thought and then asked Sir Henry if he really wanted her to come.

"Of course," replied Sir Henry, "if you won't feel smothered."

Gertrude laughed and said that, as a member of the High Commissioner's staff, she felt sexless and would, therefore, attend the banquet. This she did, wearing a new evening dress, her diamond tiara and all her orders and decorations. "Sexless," but entirely feminine.

Then when the occasion arose, the gowns and the tiaras forgotten, she would go down the Tigris with the men duck shooting, dressed in breeches and a tweed coat. She seemed to have no age, and a mind which enjoyed everything it tackled. One night she would be dining with the King advising him and discussing the intricate problems which faced him, and the next evening attending the performance of a travelling circus with the enthusiasm of a child. She rocked with laughter at the antics of the clowns and even more so at the solemn faces of the Kurdish deputies who sat together in a box and never smiled throughout the whole entertainment. Then out to Kish or Babylon, excavating, collecting and classifying the finds for the museum, and contradicting eminent archaeologists from Europe and America.

The mother of the Agha Khan, with whom Gertrude had had an amusing conversation years before in London before her name had become famous in the Orient, paid her a visit. Gertrude found the old lady to be an amazing personality, who spent her time travelling about the vast domains of Asia looking after her revered son's financial and religious interests while he raced in England.

In February of 1924 the first parliamentary elections took place. Few people believed that the Arabs, with centuries of tradition completely foreign to universal suffrage and government by the people, would ever be made to understand what this new form of administration meant. The voting was, however, carried out as if these desert people had never thought of appointing their rulers by any other method, and most of the right representatives were elected. There were ceremonies for the installation of the deputies, followed by banquets and garden parties, and the atmosphere of cordiality among all those concerned made Gertrude feel that perhaps, after all, she had not worked entirely in vain.

Her letters of this period give a feeling of lessening strain, and, in the midst of comments on what the new Government is doing, there are passages which indicate that most of the tension is over.

> "Send me out some mules (not for riding, for wearing on my feet)," she wrote to Lady Bell. "You get them at the Galleries Lafayette in Regent Street. Black and gold brocade are what I would like . . . I have been swimming vigorously and my bathing costume is wearing out and already has to be darned. Will you please get me another. The kind I like is in two pieces. I prefer silk tricotine and I like best a square or V-shaped opening at the neck. As to colour it should show a general tendency to dark blue or green, if you understand me . . ."

Lady Bell was completely baffled by this last order. Since Gertrude's last visit to England bathing suits were no longer made in two pieces or in tricotine, very few in dark blue or green. Lady Bell did her best but the garment despatched did not meet with her step-daughter's complete approval.

As if she had not already enough to do, Gertrude now started on some fresh and unofficial work. She was continually receiving inquiries from various parts of the world about the conditions in Iraq. Sometimes these queries were from an economic point of view, sometimes archaeological, often touristic. During Gertrude's earlier voyages in Persia and Asia Minor she had found that the geographical works of Strabo, compiled a little before the beginning of the Christian era, were just as accurate as twentieth century guidebooks. In many cases Strabo went into greater details than Murray and demonstrated that customs and ways of living had little changed in the Near East during the past two thousand years. In her humorous way, Gertrude decided to compile a second edition of Strabo on Iraq, and started to write a comprehensive and accurate volume in entirely "unguidebooky" style which would supply travellers with all the historical and practical details which they might require.

When she was not turning out pages of the guidebook or acting as a kind of super intelligence officer and diplomatic interviewer for the High Commissioner, she was busy in the museum. The museum was finally taking shape and, after inspecting it, the archaeologist Sir Frank Kenyon reported that he held the Iraq Department of Antiquities as a model for all departments of this kind.

But even with all these occupations Government House was always finding more things for Gertrude to do.

A Labour Government was in power in England and was inclined to be opposed to the spending of British money in Iraq. A delegation of M.P.'s was sent out to examine the situation on the spot with Lord Thomson, the Secretary of State for the Air, at the head of the commission. Lord Thomson was an abrupt man, difficult to deal with, and his colleagues were all prepared to find fault. The visit of the commission was awaited with apprehension by the people at Government House until Gertrude said that she would feel perfectly at ease with members of the Labour Party, who only needed proper handling. Sir Henry Dobbs immediately decided to take Gertrude at her word and she found herself put in charge of Lord Thomson and his companions. Gertrude treated them with her natural frankness and showed them round as if they had been ordinary visitors. She took them to see the Baghdad notables and her Arab friends and sent them back to London convinced of the wisdom of maintaining the mandate of Iraq!

This visit was followed by that of her half-sister Elsa, and her husband Admiral Richmond (later knighted), who was at that time in command of the British East Indian squadron which had come up the Persian Gulf and was anchored at Basrah. With them was their nephew George Trevelyan. Gertrude and Elsa, although separated in age by several years, had always been devoted to each other and it gave Gertrude the greatest pleasure to entertain the little party from home and introduce her Arab friends. The visit was successful beyond all expectations and a revelation to the Admiral and his staff.

The officers of the Royal Navy are the finest type of British manhood and have been responsible for planting the Union Jack in the remotest parts of the world. They have done this, however, in a detached manner, never mingling with the native populations or getting to know them. The background of conquest has always been the Wardroom, with its unbreakable traditions of the Service, and the moment a savage tribe has been subdued a cricket match has been organized to show the "damned natives" the type of people with whom they are dealing. Those Britons who have assimilated themselves to local conditions and made intimates of the inhabitants have been suspected of having "gone native."

Lady Hester Stanhope, who preceded Gertrude in a lesser degree in Arabia, adopted Eastern dress and became definitely Oriental in her way of thinking. Not so Gertrude; for, although she spoke the tribal dialects, could dine with a Bedouin or attend the banquet of an Arab king, and was known and respected all over Western Asia, she remained as fundamentally English as her brother-in-law of the Royal Navy. Her clothes came from London or Paris, she had her books sent out from Europe and her parties at her Baghdad house were given with the same formality as they would have been in her home on the Yorkshire moors.

Gertrude gave up her life to the Arab cause and died for it, but when Admiral Richmond visited her he found an Englishwoman who had retained all the dignity of her caste and treated the Arabs as her equals, because she felt that they were equal.

Slowly then the Kingdom of Iraq organized itself and settled down to a peaceful routine which enabled Gertrude to have more leisure for her excavations and her duties as head of the museum. Intensive work had been restarted in Ur, reputed to be the birthplace of Abraham but known to have existed thousands of years before, and in Kish. Kish, once the Versailles of Nebuchadnezzar, was even more ancient. Both places had been renowned for the Sumerian treasures dug up ever since archaeologists determined the sites of these two venerable cities. Gertrude had already done a great deal of work in Babylon, and, with the aid of

Professor Woolley, she now concentrated on Ur and Kish and was able to unearth some superb potteries and seals for her Baghdad museum.

But even this did not seem enough to satisfy her energy and she turned her attention to fostering a project to create a Boy Scout unit in Iraq. By the beginning of 1925 there were fifteen hundred Iraqui scouts with their own native scoutmasters, and at the end of January they were able to give a display over which Gertrude presided. Besides the ordinary scout exercises which were well carried out, a little patriotic atmosphere was introduced. The boys, dressed in the national colours, formed themselves into the flag of Iraq and then into the map of their country, with ambitious boundaries far beyond those which at that time existed. At the end of the ceremony they hoisted their flag on a tall standard and, forming a circle round it, turned towards Gertrude and cried loudly:

"Three cheers for King Faisal!"

At the end of March the organic and electoral laws were passed, and the Cabinet brought in and ratified four important measures: the dredging by the Anglo-Persian Oil Company of the mouth of the Tigris so that vessels of heavy draught could enter the port of Basrah; a trade agreement with Syria; a concession for the development of the Mosul oil fields to an international group known as the Anglo-Turkish Petroleum Company; and lastly, the drawing up of long-term contracts with some hundred British advisers whose experience would help Iraq fit herself to become an independent member of the League of Nations.

As an immediate consequence of these agreements, two British missions came out to Baghdad to examine the financial situation and the military organization of the country. The financial problems of Iraq were, to a large extent, taken over by British experts, while the military authorities adopted a scheme which would provide for a speedier training of the army so that it would shortly be able to take over the defence of the country unassisted by foreign troops.

The elections were completed by the end of June with a most satisfactory representation; the political parties which had been constituted in former years having died a natural death through the actions of Gertrude and the High Commissioners.

On July 16th, King Faisal opened Parliament in state, and, with as little fuss as if Iraq had always been ruled by a representative assembly, the government set to work to construct where destruction had always rather been the rule than the exception.

In December a new treaty between Great Britain and Iraq was submitted to Parliament and was passed almost unanimously.

Now that all Gertrude had hoped for and worked for was realized, she suddenly felt very weary. During the nine years she had been in the country she had never relaxed; rising every day at five-thirty and taking exercise till six; breakfasting at six-forty on an egg and some fruit, and being in her office by seven. The innumerable things she had to do in the office are best summed-up in her own words:

"The first thing I do in the office is to look through the three vernacular papers and translate anything that ought to be brought to the notice of the authorities. By the time I have done that papers are beginning to come in, intelligence reports from all the Near East and India, local reports, petitions, etc.

The petitions I usually dispose of myself; the local reports I note on, suggesting if necessary memoranda to the Ministers of Interior or Finance or despatches and letters. Sometimes I write a draft at once, sometimes I propose the general outlines and wait for approval or correction. In and out of all this people come in to see me, sheiks, and Arab officials, or just people who want to give some bit of information or ask for advice; if there's anything important in what they have to say I inform the High Commissioner. At intervals in the daily routine I'm now busy writing the Annual Report for the League of Nations . . ."

After a light lunch with one of her colleagues she returned to her house and rested from two-thirty till five. Then for a swim or a ride or a long walk until supper at seven-thirty, after which more work until bedtime.

And all this at the age of fifty-six when most women and many men have made up their minds that a time has come to relax and forget wearying routine. Neither could it be said that she was working for any great reward, for she knew that officially she could go no higher and financially she was out of pocket! In 1925 she recorded that her yearly expenditure exceeded her salary by £650.

But a moment came when she had to admit that even her human energy had limits of endurance. As long as she was concentrating all her energies on her mission she did not notice how run down she was, but with the reaction she realized that she was a sick woman. She accordingly decided to take a holiday and quite suddenly left Baghdad, arriving in London during August of 1925.

CHAPTER XVIII

WHEN GERTRUDE REACHED HOME, her parents realized at once that she was in a bad state of health. They called in two specialists who said that she was suffering from mental and physical exhaustion due to overwork in a pernicious climate, and declared that unless she wanted to be an invalid for life she must never return to Iraq.

Gertrude was feeling so exhausted herself that at first she accepted the doctor's recommendations and consulted several friends as to what she could do to occupy her time in England. Even in her run-down condition the thought of inactivity appalled her. It was suggested that she might stand for Parliament, and for a few days she thought the matter over. But it did not take long to put the notion out of her mind, and she wrote to the person who had made the suggestion:

"No, I'm afraid you will never see me in the House. I have an invincible hatred of that kind of politics and if you knew how little I should be fitted for it you would not give it another thought. I have not, and I never have had the quickness of thought and speech which could fit the clash of Parliament. I can do my own job in a way and explain why I think that the right way of doing it, but I don't cover a wide enough field and my natural desire is to slip back into the comfortable arena of archaeology and history, and to take only an onlooker's interest in the contest of actual affairs. I know that I could not enter the lists, apart from the fact that it would make me supremely miserable . . ."

She accordingly went up to Yorkshire, and the peaceful life in her garden and the pure air of the moors soon made her look and feel much better. She paid a visit to friends in Scotland and seemed to be drifting back into the life for which she had been brought up. But, by the time the leaves were beginning to fall, the relentless call of the East was gnawing at her again.

Her parents did their utmost to persuade her to remain at home, but Gertrude gently and firmly explained that this would be impossible. Sir Hugh and Lady Bell listened patiently, trying to understand what Gertrude meant when she said that the East had wound itself round her heart until she did not know which was herself and which was it. It seemed so strange to hear this essentially English woman affirm that she was more a citizen of Baghdad than many of the Baghdadi born. The ecstasy in her eyes as she spoke of the loveliness of the Tigris and the palm trees along its banks, of the magnificence of the desert and the charm of the Arabs, seemed foreign to a woman born and bred in Yorkshire.

"You see," she would say with emotion, "I lost the opportunity to make a home of my own a long time ago, and these people have taken the place of a family. They need me, they come to me for comfort and encouragement and in their comfort I find my own. I feel limited in this country which you could never leave, and my whole being longs for that vast, merciless desert which must be my home until the end . . ."

The parents saw that there was no argument which would alter Gertrude's decision, they made the most of her remaining days in England, and at the end of October 1925 said goodbye to her as she set out on her last journey to the land of the Arabs. She, however, compromised to the extent of taking with her as a companion her first cousin Sylvia Henley, the daughter of Lord Sheffield.

Back in Baghdad, Gertrude was welcomed as though she had risen from the dead. She had hardly begun to unpack when streams of Iraquis were pouring into her garden . . . "Light of our eyes," they cried, "light of our eyes . . ." as they kissed her hands. And Gertrude felt grateful that she had had the strength to come back to the people who needed her.

Almost immediately King Faisal returned from the trip which he had made to Europe, and arrived by plane. The Cabinet and dignitaries of Baghdad, with the High Commissioner and his staff, were at the aerodrome to meet him. The King's plane appeared on the desert horizon, escorted by nine smaller planes, and landed outside the oasis where the reception took place. It was all very formal and matter of fact, and no one seemed to regard it as miraculous or peculiar that the descendant of the Prophet should alight on his kingdom from the air. Yet there were many present at that aerodrome who, ten years earlier, would have fled at the sight of an airplane, supposing it to be a genie! Gertrude dropped her curtsey, and the King, as usual, made a point of singling her out from the people who were meeting him.

The New Year of 1926 was very unhappy for Gertrude as her half-brother Hugo, to whom she was devoted, died in England of typhoid. She had but lately lost her uncle Lord Sheffield, to whom she was devoted, and Sylvia Henley had found the climate of Baghdad too much for her and had been obliged to return to Europe. These losses seemed to crush Gertrude and had an undoubted effect on her health, which, from now on, deteriorated. She had bouts of fever and sleepless nights interspersed with terrifying nightmares, during which all that she had been through in Iraq and Arabia came back in grotesque form. She gave herself no chance to recuperate, and continued her political duties as well as those connected with the museum.

A spacious building had now been set aside to store Gertrude's finds and she was kept busy planning the rooms and sorting out all that had been collected. When all was ready the King opened the museum and the following day the public was admitted. A curious public, which went to the museum because Gertrude had made it, but quite vague in their minds as to why the bits of pottery and old seals should be given a fine home and looked upon with such respect. From time immemorial these remains of the past had been within the reach of every Arab beggar and had been regarded as so many old stones.

Mrs. Harold Nicolson came to stay with Gertrude and was one of the last of her old friends to see her alive. Writing in her book *A Passenger to Tehran*, she said:

". . . Then a door in the blank wall, a jerky stop, a creaking of hinges, a broadly smiling servant, a rush of dogs, a vision of the garden path edged with carnations in pots, a little low house at the end of the path, an English voice—Gertrude Bell . . .

". . . Then she was back in her chair pouring out information, the state of Iraq, the excavations at Ur, the need for a bigger museum, what new books had come out? What was happening in England? The doctors had told her she ought not to go through another summer in Baghdad, but what could she do in England eating out her heart for Iraq? Next year perhaps . . .

but I couldn't say she looked ill, could I? I could and did! She laughed and brushed that aside . . .

". . . She was a wonderful hostess, and I felt that her personality held together and made a centre for all those exiled Englishmen whose other common bond was their service of Iraq. They all seemed to be instilled by the same spirit of constructive enthusiasm; but I could not help feeling that their mission there would have been more in a nature of drudgery than of zeal, but for the radiant ardour of Gertrude Bell. Whatever subject she touched, she lit up; such vitality was irresistible. We laid plans, alas! for when I should return to Baghdad in the autumn; we would go to Babylon, we would go to Ctesiphon, she would have got her new museum by then. When she went back to England, if, indeed she was compelled to go, she would write another book . . . So we sat talking, as friends talk who have not seen one another for a long time, until the shadows lengthened and she said it was time to go and see the King . . ."

As if Fate had decided that something more must be done to wear out the stubborn vitality of this obstinate English-woman, Gertrude suddenly had another onerous duty thrown upon her shoulders. Terrific rains caused the Tigris to overflow its banks, bringing disaster to all the neighbouring country. The Government immediately called on Gertrude, and she found herself serving on the committee of relief for the flood sufferers and, as usual, having to do practically everything in this connection. But she treated it as being all in the day's work and merely commented:

"I also find it boring, for all the desert where I used to ride and walk is a lake . . . the Ark and all the rest become quite comprehensible when one sees Mesopotamia in flood time."

And so her work continued throughout the torrid summer in Baghdad. Gertrude's letters did not indicate to her parents that she was feeling ill, but there was a certain note of weariness underlying the usual enthusiastic accounts of what was going on.

The last great event in the development of the destinies of Iraq which seemed to predict an era of permanent peace was the signing of the tripartite treaty between Great Britain, Turkey and Iraq. The treaty was ratified by the two chambers of the Iraq Parliament on June 14, 1926, and on June 25th the King gave a banquet to celebrate the event. Gertrude was one of the principal guests at the party and appeared radiantly happy at the fulfilment of her hopes and dreams. Her belief in Faisal and the Arab people had been justified, her perseverance had been rewarded.

This was the last State function which she attended. She was not actually ill, but she wanted to be alone and remained more and more among the rose trees of her garden which spread mantles of rioting colour over the walls. The scents of the flowers seemed to soothe her and carried her back to another rose-dressed house in the East where she had first listened to a dear, long dead voice which had opened her mind to the treasures of the Orient. The voice seemed nearer now and she waited almost impatiently for the time, which she knew was fast approaching, when she could go to the refuge of those loving arms.

On the morning of July 12th she did not get up at her usual early hour and an unaccustomed silence brooded over her home. When her servants became worried and went into her room to see if their mistress was unwell, they found her dead. That vital flame which nothing had ever quenched had flickered out as she passed peacefully away in her sleep.

* * *

Gertrude's death caused widespread sorrow throughout the United Kingdom and Britain's Empire beyond the seas. To the general public she had become a legendary personality, to the Government one of those servants of the State who could not be replaced, to her family the daughter who, while giving her life to her country, never for one day forgot home.

From all over England and her Dominions came letters and telegrams of sympathy. No particular class was represented by the mourners. Ministers of State, men of letters, archaeologists, soldiers and sailors, villagers of the North Country, grieved that they had lost Gertrude Bell.

The Colonial Secretary spoke of Gertrude's death and her work for Britain before a crowded and silent House of Commons.

George the Fifth of England wrote to Gertrude's parents:

> "The Queen and I are grieved to hear of the death of your distinguished daughter whom we held in high regard.
>
> "The nation will mourn with us the loss of one who by her intellectual powers, force of character and personal courage rendered important and what I trust will prove lasting benefit to the country and to those regions where she worked with such devotion and self sacrifice. We truly sympathise with you in your sorrow.
>
> "George R. I."

In the Arab countries there was grief and consternation. Gertrude was idolized in the minds of the desert people as someone above all others, a creature who could not die, a person without whom they felt that life would no longer be the same.

Letters from all parts of Arabia, Syria, Palestine and Iraq, on all kinds of paper, in all manner of calligraphy, flooded the offices of the High Commissioner. The highest and the lowest tried to express their grief and convey their gratitude for all that Gertrude had done for them. Some of the letters were veritable poems, some just incoherent words of sorrow. There were so many that their publication would have filled a book.

One of the most touching of these missives came from old Haji Naji in whose garden Gertrude had so often rested from her work. There were just two lines:

> "It was my faith always to send to Miss Bell the first of my fruits and vegetables and I know not now where I shall send them."

Gertrude's funeral ceremony was a magnificent apotheosis to her life. A torrid day had ended with one of those golden evenings of the desert. A warm breeze rustled through the tall palm trees of the oasis and ruffled the sluggish waters of the Tigris. Placed in a plain wooden coffin Gertrude's body moved slowly through the silent streets of Baghdad which were thronged with robed figures who made no attempt to conceal their feelings. Along the route, over which Gertrude had so often walked and ridden, the troops of the Iraq army "rested on arms reversed" as the long procession passed. The High Commissioner and Prime Minister followed the hearse as chief mourners, and behind them all the members of the Iraq Cabinet and the British civil, military and air force staffs. The full-dress uniforms of the Englishmen glistened white in the sunset and contrasted with the bronzed faces which had lost their proverbial British imperturbability.

Close on the heels of the officials came a host of tall, dark-skinned men in flowing garments, their turbans bound about with strands of black camel hair interwoven with threads of silver and gold. The Sheiks of Arabia had come to pay their last tribute to the woman with whom they had wandered about the desert and for whom not one would have hesitated to give his life. Proudly and silently they strode, but, like their British companions, their faces had lost that haughty indifference of men of great lineage.

From the gates of the cemetery the coffin was borne to the graveside by those young men of the High Commissioner's staff who had worked with Gertrude and to whom her home had been a haven of rest in the midst of a strange and often hostile people. The coffin was draped in the Union Jack on which rested Gertrude's many orders and decorations.

Before the words of commitment, Sir Henry Dobbs stepped forward. His eyes were strained as he looked about him, at the Englishmen in their uniforms and the Arabs in their robes. Speaking clearly, but without the formal authority of his usual speeches, he said:

"For the last ten years of her life, Gertrude Bell concentrated all the indomitable fervour of her spirit and all the astounding gifts of her mind, to the service of the Arab cause, and especially to Iraq. At last her body, always frail, was broken by the energy of her soul. Her bones rest where she had wished them to rest: in the soil of Iraq. Her friends are left desolate."

The High Commissioner saluted the coffin and stepped back.

"Man, that is born of a woman, hath but a short time to

live, and is full of misery . . . he fleeth as it were a shadow, and never continueth in one stay . . . In the midst of life we are in death . . . earth to earth, ashes to ashes, dust to dust; in sure and certain hope of the Resurrection . . ."

The firing party raised their rifles, there was a sharp word of command and the three volleys crackled out in the still air. The sad, heartrending notes of the Last Post swelled up and died away. After a pause the buglers once more placed the bugles to their lips and hopefully the Reveille went echoing through the oasis. As the people turned sadly away, the sun dipped in flaming orange behind the wastes of the desert and sent a shaft of emerald green light into the sky. The breeze freshened and went whispering through the feathery palm trees as they gracefully bowed to one whom they had watched over for so many years. The palm trees of the neighbouring oasis took up the message and passed it on until the rustling died softly in another oasis hundreds of miles away beside the grave of a young man to whose memory a very noble lady had remained faithful for over thirty years.

So Gertrude sleeps on, on the rising ground outside Baghdad. At her feet the Tigris rolls sluggishly along, and away the desert stretches out in its barren immensity. A simple white stone with the name in English and in Arabic marks the grave.

In Baghdad the principal wing of the museum bears Gertrude's name, this last token to her memory being at the immediate request of King Faisal.

A brass plaque in the wall states:

GERTRUDE BELL

Whose memory the Arabs will ever hold in reverence and affection created this museum in 1923.

King Faisal and the Government of Iraq in gratitude for her great deeds in this country have ordered that the principal wing shall bear her name.

* * *

It was spring on the Yorkshire moors. The mauve and green of the heather had the freshness of rebirth under the golden rays of the setting sun. A blackcock called as he scanned the sky for a late hunting hawk; a cock grouse strutted importantly before the chicks which boldly ventured from beneath the wings of their anxious mother; a dog fox waited hungrily until man and hound had observed that curious ritual of retiring to bed when the hunting was at its best.

The world tipped quickly up, caressed the flaming disk of the sun and took it to herself. The afterglow died and the twilight came, accentuating the whiteness of the moorland road along which a man came striding as one accustomed to long marches. He wore the khaki uniform of a British soldier, and on his chest the ribbons commemorating wars in distant parts contrasted with the drabness of his tunic.

As the soldier reached the crest of the road he paused and turned towards the west. He had not seen a sunset over these wild moors for years and he remained feasting his eyes on the greens and the purples and the browns as they gradually faded with the oncoming darkness. He had purposely walked from the station so that he could relish alone this scene which he had so often conjured up in his mind during his service in the East. The spring night rushed on, extinguishing the colours until the countryside became a great, rolling, hueless expanse. It suddenly reminded the watcher of the desert and carried his mind back to days long ago when he used to sit with his father outside the moorland cottage and hear of the strange lands where the flag of England had led him. In those days the acres over which Mr. Bell's gamekeeper watched had seemed to the boy the vastest territory he could visualize. He smiled now as the memories of the immensity of the desert floated before his mind.

It was quite dark when the soldier resumed his trudge. The wind rose and whispered through the heather and stirred up little clouds of dust on the road. Down there he could see twinkling lights which beckoned a welcome. Coming home made his periods of exile worth while, but this time he had a sacred mission to perform before he crossed the threshold of his mother's cottage . . .

After a while the moorland gave way to a few straggling houses and then to a church. An evening service was coming to an end and the stained-glass windows stood out blue and red against the night. The soldier waited until the bulk of the congregation had disappeared, and entering the church he avoided the main aisle and made his way up the side, looking for something. He ignored the verger, who was putting out the lights, and attentively examined each window in turn. Finally he stopped before a lovely piece of glass. His eyes drank in the soft colours and then rested on an inscription in Persian. He could not decipher the characters but they gave him a happy sense of familiarity and he stared at them affectionately before turning to the English translation:

Thus said the poet: "When death comes to you
All ye whose life-sand through the hour-glass slips,
He lays two fingers on your ears, and two
Upon your eyes he lays, one on your lips;
Whispering, 'Silence!' "[1]

And then below the verse his eyes came to more words:

To the memory of Gertrude Bell.

The soldier automatically came to "attention"; then, fumbling in his tunic, he took out an envelope which he carefully opened. A dried and faded Persian rose lay in his hands which he gently smoothed and reverently laid on the sill of the window. For another minute he remained reading the inscription, then turned and walked slowly through the darkened church; and as he went he seemed to feel a host of robed figures crowding about him and filling the church with all the scents of the East.

Out on the moors all was quiet, the only signs of life were the lights of the Yorkshire iron foundries flickering in the distance like the fires of Arab camps in the desert.

[1] This is Gertrude's English adaptation from one of her favourite Persian poems and is carved round her memorial window in the village church of her home in Yorkshire.

INDEX

REDWOOD LIBRARY AND ATHENAEUM
3 693 300 132798 B

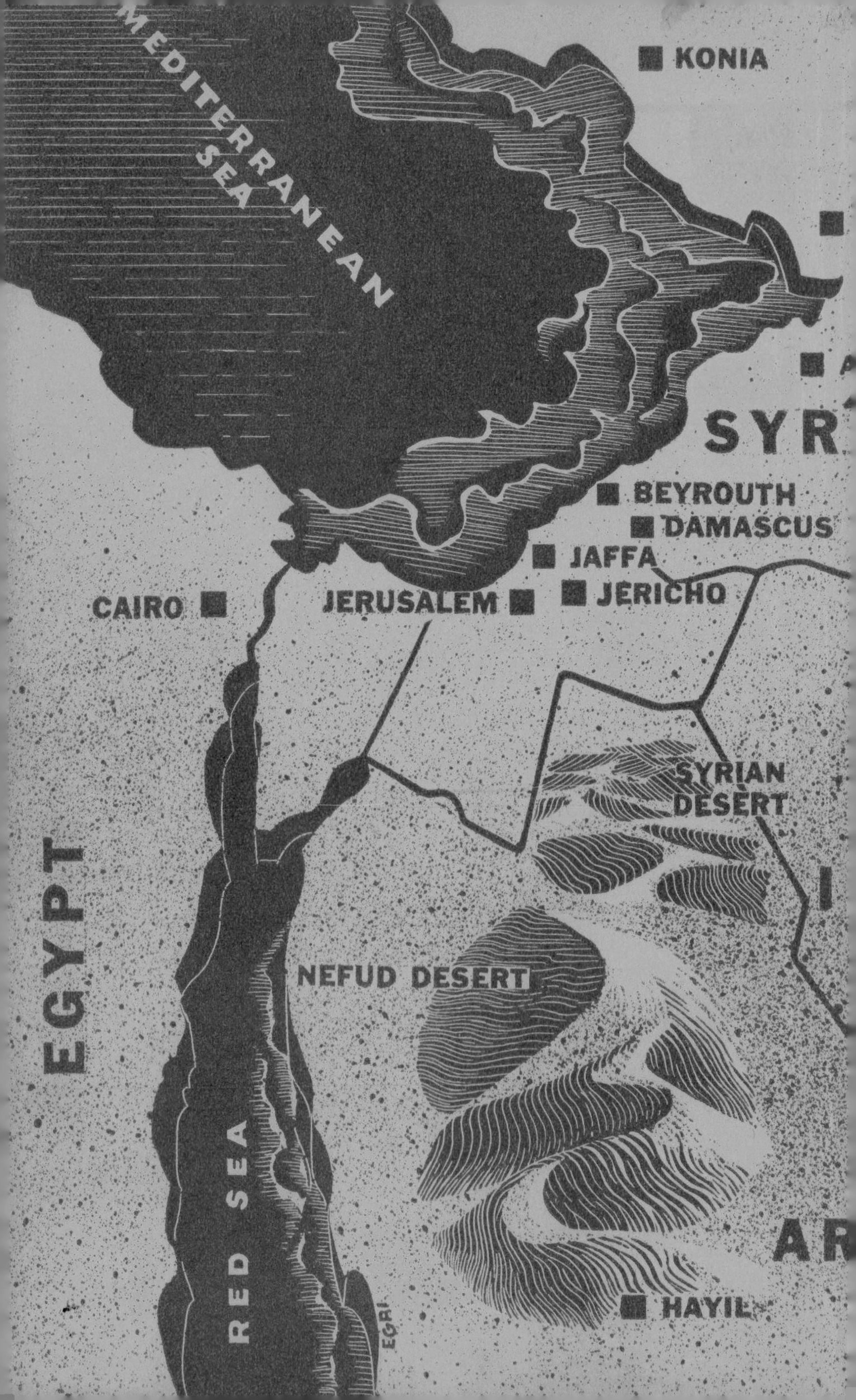
MEDITERRANEAN SEA
KONIA
SYR
BEYROUTH
DAMASCUS
JAFFA
CAIRO
JERUSALEM
JERICHO
SYRIAN DESERT
EGYPT
NEFUD DESERT
RED SEA
AR
HAYIL
EGRI